What Is
Spiritual Freedom?

Also by Harold Klemp

Ask the Master, Book 1
Ask the Master, Book 2
Child in the Wilderness
The Living Word
Soul Travelers of the Far Country
The Spiritual Exercises of ECK
The Temple of ECK
The Wind of Change

The Mahanta Transcripts Series

Journey of Soul, Book 1
How to Find God, Book 2
The Secret Teachings, Book 3
The Golden Heart, Book 4
Cloak of Consciousness, Book 5
Unlocking the Puzzle Box, Book 6
The Eternal Dreamer, Book 7
The Dream Master, Book 8
We Come as Eagles, Book 9
The Drumbeat of Time, Book 10

Stories to Help You See
God in Your Life

The Book of ECK Parables, Volume 1
The Book of ECK Parables, Volume 2
The Book of ECK Parables, Volume 3
The Book of ECK Parables, Volume 4

What Is
Spiritual Freedom?

Harold Klemp

Mahanta Transcripts
Book 11

ECKANKAR
Minneapolis, MN

What Is Spiritual Freedom?
Mahanta Transcripts, Book 11

Copyright © 1995 ECKANKAR

Printed in U.S.A.

Compiled by Mary Carroll Moore
Edited by Joan Klemp and Anthony Moore

Cover design by Lois Stanfield
Cover illustration by Barbara Moss
Text illustrations by Signy Cohen
Text photo (page xii) by Robert Huntley
Back cover photo by Robert Huntley

Library of Congress Cataloging-in-Publication Data

Klemp, Harold.
     What is spiritual freedom? / Harold Klemp.
        p. cm. — (Mahanta transcripts ; bk. 11)
     Includes index.
     ISBN 1-57043-101-9 : $14.00
     1. Eckankar (Organization)—Doctrines. 2. Spiritual life.
   I. Title. II. Series: Klemp, Harold. Mahanta transcripts ; bk. 11.
   BP605.E3K577 1995
   299'.93—dc20   94-42227
                                                           CIP

Soul's Voyage to Spiritual Freedom

We ride the stormy ocean of life, fighting the sea, wind, and towering waves. The journey, full of peril, seems endless.

Then the clear Light of God streams through the storm clouds of daily living. It sheds the light of truth. It is Divine Spirit, the ECK.

Our battered ship has finally made its way to the calm waters of spiritual freedom. Now our journey may continue with purpose and direction.

—Sri Harold Klemp

Contents

of Activity • Understanding Another's Truth • You Can't Follow Two Masters • A Natural Transition to ECK • Spiritual Experience • Where Is That Light? • Finding Proof • Stages of Spiritual Growth • Holy Moment • Why Tell Stories?

Foreword

The Way of the Eternal, *The Shariyat-Ki-Sugmad,* Book One, states: "The knowledge that the true, living Master gives is direct and immediate, coming from actual Soul experiences apart from the physical senses and human consciousness. His words are charged with the ECK currents surging within him. They sink into the inner self of the listener, leaving little doubt about the existence of Soul experiences."

Sri Harold Klemp, the Mahanta, the Living ECK Master travels in all parts of the world to give the sacred teachings of ECK. Many of his public talks have been released on audiocassette, but others have never before been available beyond the particular seminar at which he spoke.

As a special service to the students of ECK and truth seekers everywhere, all of Sri Harold's public talks are being transcribed and edited under his direction. Now these transcripts can be study aids for your greater spiritual understanding.

What Is Spiritual Freedom? Mahanta Transcripts, Book 11, contains his talks from 1991–92. May they serve to uplift you to a greater vision of life.

Sri Harold Klemp, the Mahanta, the Living ECK Master helps people to see the small, secret ways life leads each Soul toward greater spiritual freedom.

1

A Great Love for God, Part 1

Each time I prepare a seminar talk, I wonder, *What can I say that will be of any help to those of you who come? What will help you spiritually?*

New Look at Karma

Sometimes people ask me, "What do you have to offer in ECKANKAR? How are you different from Christianity?"

I tell them about karma and reincarnation.

Generally people think of karma as something bad. They never think of it as possibly something good—for example, the three-year-old child who plays the piano brilliantly.

Sometimes karma isn't as much what you do; it's where you are. You happen to be in the wrong place at the wrong time because you didn't know better. When good things happen to you, it's often just the right time and right place.

Mouse Story

This summer I had my birdseed out in the garage. One evening, I went to refill the feeder. A cardinal, a pretty little red-orange bird, always comes to the bird feeder and makes a racket if I'm late with the evening feed.

That evening it was dark in the garage, and I was in a hurry. I opened the bag of birdseed, stuck my hand in, and fished around with the plastic quart container I use to scoop the seed. Suddenly I felt a mouse running around in the bag trying to keep away from my hand. It startled both of us.

The mouse jumped out of the bag and ran out of the garage. It had upset me, and I had upset it.

The mouse was having dinner, minding its own business, when suddenly someone turned on the light and came fishing around in its dinner, trying to catch its tail.

I was sorry this had upset the mouse, but I decided that I couldn't allow it to be running around in the bag of birdseed. So I went to the hardware store to buy a mousetrap.

A Better Way

At the hardware store I looked at mousetraps. They had the kind that I knew as a child—the kind that are very hard on mice. *There must be a better way,* I thought, so I looked around some more until I found a very clever device called a humane mousetrap.

This mousetrap plays on the mouse's curiosity.

Out of curiosity, the mouse goes into a tunnel and steps on a little treadle. This treadle sets off a tiny paddle wheel—similar to ones on the back of riverboats. The wheel swipes the mouse into a little shoe box, and there the mouse is supposed to stay until you come and let him go in the great forest.

When I got home, I set the mousetrap on top of the bag of birdseed. The instructions said to wind it up, but not too tightly. When I went into the garage the next day, there was evidence of the mouse's worry in the bottom of the box. But the mouse had escaped.

Although I had followed the instructions carefully, I hadn't wound the spring tightly enough. Evidently when the mouse got into the box, he just pushed the paddle back and walked out.

This time I wound the mousetrap really tight. A couple of days later I found more evidence of a mouse having been in the box. But there was still no mouse inside. Finally I figured it out: wind the spring just a couple of turns so it didn't damage the trap but still kept the mouse inside.

I adjusted it and made sure the little paddle wheel closed up the opening very nicely, then I set it out once more.

In a day or so I finally found the first little mouse. It was sitting in the corner, shaking. I told it, "Better this trap than the other one," and I carried it out to the forest and let it go. A day later, the mouse's child came out looking for Mom. So I carried it out to the forest too, and I hope they found each other.

These mice were in the wrong place at the wrong time, but I had the right equipment. We were thus able to both live peacefully. I reclaimed my home, and they found a new one in the great forest.

Cause and Effect

This is cause and effect.

The mouse had been smart for weeks: I'd found seed scattered around the garage, but I couldn't figure out how it got there. It never occurred to me that there'd be a mouse in my very clean garage. When I found a hole gnawed through the side of the seed bag, I got suspicious. "Somebody's here who shouldn't be," I said. Then the mouse crossed the line, and we ran into each other in the seed bag. I had to figure out a way to take care of the problem. So I got the mousetrap.

Mark Twain said that if a cat sits on a hot stove once, he won't sit there twice. I still use a flashlight when I look in the seed bag these days. I won't stick my hand in that bag of seed again without first looking for a mouse.

Most people are that way. We get into problems or mischief. Then things go wrong in our lives, and we generally go get the problem fixed. We go to some expert, and he helps us. We go to the doctor to get ourselves fixed up; we go to the banker and take out a loan. But unless we can learn what caused that problem in the first place, we'll probably continue to repeat it again and again until we figure out what's going on. Then we can finally get it right.

Greater Side of God

In the last few years I've been trying to show people a greater side of themselves. To do this, I have to show them a greater side of God. This is not very easy.

ECKANKAR has two aspects: the inner and the outer teachings.

These are very distinct from each other, and yet they are also part of the same teaching. The outer teachings are what you read in an ECK book or hear from me or another ECKist about the principles of ECK.

Every so often I will put attention on the inner teachings for a year or two. The esoteric side of ECKANKAR includes the dream teachings. This is one of the ways you can learn the higher truths of God and the Holy Spirit.

Soul Travel is another one of the esoteric teachings. Soul Travel simply means that you as Soul are moving into a higher state of awareness.

Self-Responsibility

When my daughter graduated from high school, I was so grateful. As a child's graduation approaches, the parent often says, "Please, God, let it happen." When it happens, the parent says, "Truly, I have much to be thankful for." We love our children.

I've never been one to hold on to my daughter. I always wanted her to grow up. Ever since she was five, I've told her, "Being a kid isn't any fun. You're going to have me on your case all the time. By the time you're eighteen, I've got to make sure that you know how to fit into this world. I've got to make sure you know your way around. When you do something, you need to know what this society expects from you. I have to make sure that by the time you reach eighteen, when you do something wrong you don't say, 'Gee, I didn't know.' "

We as parents are teaching our children to become aware, throughout their childhood, of what it means to be a responsible person in society. In the same way, it's my job in ECKANKAR to show those people who come to the teachings of ECK how to be responsible and mature spiritual beings.

Judgment Day

People say Armageddon's coming — a final battle between the forces of good and evil on Judgment Day. The last day. The day it doesn't pay to buy a lottery ticket. When I was young, the idea of the Judgment Day used to frighten me. People will start saying it more as we get nearer to the year 2000. As if God cares about our man-made calendar.

When the wall came down between the East and West, and the United States and the Soviets began putting their powerful toys back in the toy box, some people began to say, "Now we shall have world peace." I said, "No, we're just having a breather for a minute. It's going to pop up somewhere else."

These problems people always have with other people will pop up. There are going to be little wars, then bigger wars.

Gift of Spiritual Awareness

My job is to help you become more aware of what you do and why what happens to you is of your own making.

If ECKANKAR has anything to offer you, it is full responsibility for whatever you do. No one's going to come along and save you from yourself. But on the other hand, nobody is going to hold the last day over you either.

I find it interesting that even in Christ's time his own disciples felt that the Judgment Day would come before they died. Christ said, "There be some standing here, which shall not taste of death, till they see the kingdom of God."

But Christ was speaking of the esoteric side, the inner teachings. Of course, people being people—having to live in a very practical, hard world—they took everything at face value. They thought he meant there was going to be a Judgment Day when the sky would split open and Christ would come down on a cloud.

It was hard on some people when the first man walked on the moon or when the first rocket put a satellite into orbit. For the first time, puny humankind was now taking a step into God's territory. This was where someday angels would blow trumpets, come down on a cloud, and tell you, "Hey, it's all over. Forget your things, leave the bread in the oven; it doesn't matter anymore." But as soon as the first satellite went into outer space—as soon as the cameras began taking pictures of us down here—we began to look pretty insignificant. We looked pretty small and foolish.

Putting Love into Action

In America, we pride ourselves that we stand for freedom. But in many areas we don't have complete freedom. It's impossible.

If you put two people in a room, suddenly you've got problems with each person's privacy. In a country, this means one culture is often pushing on another culture. People today are very incensed about how the Europeans pushed out the Native Americans. But before the Europeans came, the Native Americans were busy pushing each other around.

This is the nature of people.

In ECKANKAR, we believe in karma. The last day, the Judgment Day, is happening to us every day. The difference is that we know it. We have good things coming to us; we also have other experiences coming to us.

Who's to say what's right and what's not, what's meaningful for each person? The only one who can do that for you is you, because you are Soul.

You are made in the image of God. And being made in the image of God, you share the attributes of God. The greatest of these are freedom, power, and divine love, or charity. Charity and divine love are similar. Charity is love put into motion in everyday life.

Why Did This Happen to Me?

I try to help people become more aware of who and what they are.

Sometimes I work with them in the dream state, sometimes with Soul Travel. Sometimes we work with other aspects of ECK that you have an interest in or—if this is what you are supposed to do spiritually—even such things as the gift of prophecy. I don't encourage it though because many people use it to have power and control over others.

I put attention on day-to-day life. This is where people are having a hard time understanding things.

They wonder, Why did I get fired? When you get fired, when you get sick, or when anything else happens, the conditioned human response is to begin blaming others.

We say, "The reason this happened to me is because of that person there." Why? Because we've been babied into thinking that somebody's going to pick up after us spiritually for the rest of our lives. We make a mistake, no problem. Somebody will fix it for us. But this isn't true.

Mysterious Hay Fever

A couple of months ago I was having lunch with my wife and two ECK initiates. We went to a restaurant, and they brought us some flowers. It was very nice of them.

My wife and I met with these two ECKists again a couple of months later. This time each of them had brought us a single rose. The meal was just about finished when one said, "I don't understand why every time we have lunch with you I get hay fever."

As clear as a flash I saw what the problem was. I said, "Next time you have lunch with us, don't bring any flowers."

The woman was allergic to these flowers. On the drive over she held them in her lap, right under her nose. This hay fever wasn't because she was meeting me; it was because of the flowers.

Popcorn

A close friend got stomach ulcers. She called one day to talk to my wife and mentioned this.

People think I get the answer to problems right off the top of my head. Actually, I sift through the situation, then I get an idea. "Ask her if she's eating anything like potato chips or pretzels," I said to my wife.

"She isn't eating any of those things," my wife reported back the next time she talked to our friend. "But she does eat a lot of popcorn."

We think of popcorn as nice fluffy stuff, but if you look carefully you can see that it has sharp hulls. For some people, these hulls act like little saws inside. I found out later our friend was eating two and a half gallons of popcorn a day. She didn't even realize she was eating so much.

So I told my wife, "Next time you talk with her, suggest that she cut back on the popcorn. Suggest that she find an amount that she can eat without it hurting her."

But the ECKist felt it couldn't be popcorn. So she kept eating it.

Soon her stomach problem was very serious. She went to a clinic, and the doctor prescribed a very strong medicine. Then she had a reaction to that medicine, so the doctor put her on something else. The second medicine caused problems in the joints. So the doctor gave her a third prescription. Soon this ECKist was taking three medicines to take care of her popcorn.

This person is very bright and perceptive. She's one of the most spiritually aware people I've ever met. I mention this lest we get too proud of our own abilities and awareness. Like this woman, we think (1) it couldn't be because of the popcorn, and (2) if it were due to the popcorn, we would have figured it out before now.

I can almost guarantee you this: 99 percent of the time you won't be able to figure out your own problem. It's too close to you, and you've invested a lot in it. For instance, popcorn makes you feel good. It's something that makes your life enjoyable. You'll fight anyone who wants to take your popcorn away from you.

Becoming Aware

Becoming aware of who and what we are is a very gradual process.

Why do we care about food? Because when we're hurting from what we're eating, we can't enjoy life. We can't enjoy the good things of life. And we should enjoy them. We should be able to work and have good things for ourselves and our families. So if there are things hurting us, we should find out why. Is there a pattern? Is this an old problem coming up again or one that is similar but not quite the same?

Look more deeply into these problems you have, and you'll probably find a common thread. How do you begin unwinding it?

People are sometimes like bunches of string lying on the floor. There are all kinds of knots that twist and tie through these bunches of string. Karma is untying each one of these knots and working a way through the bunch of string that is you. No one is going to take your problems away from you.

Someday you're going to have to face yourself and work your way into a better life. It's up to you.

Healings from HU

HU is the name of God that some of you have learned to sing. Sometimes when you're very ill, you can sing HU-U-U-U.

Sing it quietly to yourself or silently inside. You may get a healing of some sort. Someone may just walk up to you and mention something that tells you to go to a certain doctor, chiropractor, dentist, optometrist, whatever. This particular doctor may not be the one. You may have to go to two or three, but it's a beginning.

When you sing HU, this name for God, you're saying, "I open myself to the will of God. Not as I will, but as Thou wilt." You look to some direction higher than yourself. Prayer is good as long as people use it for gratitude, for thanking God for their blessings.

It's OK to pray for healings too. But sometimes we eat too much ice cream, end up with abscessed teeth, and then pray to God to take away the problem. When this happened to me, my gums had been warning me for months with twinges. My body was saying, "Too much sugar; we can't handle that, slow down." Your body will tell you many times when you're doing too much of something. It doesn't matter that your friends eat a quart of ice cream or two and a half gallons of popcorn a day. You're totally different, a unique being. There is no one else like you.

You Are Soul

You do not have a Soul; you are Soul.
This is where the teachings of ECK are more direct

11

and more honest. When you say, "I am Soul," you are recognizing that you are indeed a child of God. You share in the divine attributes and qualities of God. All you have to do is recognize them. You just need to be aware of who and what you are.

Some people grow up in a religion with a very materialistic viewpoint: my car, my house, my wife, my husband, my wallet, my credit cards, my children, my Soul.

Well, where do you keep this Soul? In your wallet? Are you saying that Soul is a material possession that you can actually possess, have, and hold? Then who are you? Who's talking? Mind? Emotions? Or just flesh? Is that all you are?

If I can leave you with one thing—something that will help you open into a greater state of awareness—it is this: Simply recognize that you are Soul. You do not have a Soul; you are Soul.

If you can let this sink in a little, you'll begin to understand that this is what makes you special.

The Divinity of All

And if you let it sink in a little more, you'll begin to understand that it makes every other human being special too. Because Soul is Soul. You are Soul, your spouse is Soul, your children are Soul.

When you recognize yourself as being divine in origin and recognize this same divinity in others, only then can you begin to love truly. And when you begin to love truly, you begin to live truly.

I'm not saying that just because you come into ECK life is going to be easy street. That every lottery ticket you buy will have a winning number. That all your ships will come in. I can't say that. Those of you who have been in

ECK know that sometimes when you begin to face your-self, life can get even harder than it was before. You have a little catching up to do. You begin working off karma, the debts you have created against yourself.

A way to help yourself through this is to sing HU.

When you go to sleep at night, try to remember your dreams. Once you recognize that you are Soul and you know how to sing HU, your dreams will begin to have significance in your life. I say it this way purposely: Your dreams will begin to have significance. It doesn't mean you're going to understand them right away. At first, dreams can be wonderfully jumbled.

This summer we went to Africa. It was the first time I'd been there since 1987. There were ten thousand people at the seminar, and we all sang HU. I don't often sing HU with the audience. But when ten thousand of us sang it in Africa, it was memorable.

Love Song from the Heart

Whenever I go to Africa, I love to hear them sing. They accept life more on its terms than perhaps we in the West do.

We have so many things isolating us from life, so many conveniences. We don't like to sweat; we don't like to wait. We like to hurry and get a lot of things done. We like to make our computers really hum so we can run two or three programs at once. And at the end of the day we feel good if we've crammed more in than it's right to do.

In Africa, the people are sometimes closer to life. When they sing their love song to God, it comes from their hearts. In the West when we sing, it often comes from our minds. This is not an advantage because the teachings of ECK are the teachings of the heart.

The mind is just a little box, a little humane mousetrap we play with. We wind it up; we watch it spin. It really doesn't do much to uplift us spiritually.

But the song of HU can.

*ECK Worldwide Seminar, Minneapolis, Minnesota,
Friday, October 25, 1991*

No matter what you do in life, if you can just love what you're doing and see the gift of God in little things, you'll be happy.

2

A Great Love for God, Part 2

Summer's over, and the mosquitoes are now only a bad memory. They're bad karma for us in summer, it is good karma for us in fall when they leave—even though we know they're just lying around waiting to reincarnate in spring.

Dragonflies and Mosquitoes

I saw an advertisement for a little electronic device that makes a sound like a dragonfly. The ad said dragonflies are the mortal enemy of mosquitoes. "Be safe from mosquitoes!" it said.

Since we had a trip to Africa planned for this summer, I thought the device might be a good thing to take along. They have different insects there who haven't tasted me yet and might consider me a delicacy. So I bought a few—then remembered on the plane that I'd forgotten to pack them.

When I got home from the trip, I was eager to try these things out. Feeling kind of foolish, I hung one of them around my neck. Then I figured if I was going to try these things, I might as well do it right—so I put on two and went outside.

The device was making a peculiar noise, a clicking sound like dragonflies supposedly make. The instructions had said that it's best to use the device in a quiet area where noise doesn't drown out the click. So I was out watering the flowers and feeding the birds, and the mosquitoes were just tearing into me.

"This thing isn't working," I said. "Maybe we have mosquitoes who are hard of hearing."

Then I realized the water from the hose was drowning out the sound. So I turned off the hose. And the next thing I knew, a dragonfly flew over to me. The dragonfly kept trying to come closer and closer. This wasn't exactly what I had in mind when I bought the devices.

I went inside and told my wife what had happened. "I can't use these things," I said. That week we got two more of them in the mail from an ECK friend. So I sat one in the window by my desk. One day I noticed a dragonfly buzzing around the screen.

The device didn't repel mosquitoes, but it did a good job attracting dragonflies.

No matter what you do in life, if you can just love what you're doing and see the gift of God in little things, you'll be happy. To me, the dragonfly coming over was a big thing. It doesn't take much to keep me happy.

Eighth Initiation Question

An ECKist brought me a blue jacket from Hong Kong. I've had it nine years, and I wear it all the time while I do yard work. I throw it in the wash, and it doesn't fade. Cotton that will not lose its colors says something about the makers of the jacket. "Those Chinese have something to teach us," I said to the ECKist.

She recently got her Eighth Initiation. It's hard for anyone to get. We took her to a restaurant afterward, and

I encouraged her to get dessert. "It's a big day," I said. So she ordered a piece of cheesecake.

She ate half then got to thinking about her coworker back at the ECKANKAR Spiritual Center. So she decided to take half the cheesecake back to her friend and asked the waiter for a take-out box.

While we were waiting, the ECKist said to me, "My friend asked me what it takes to get the Eighth Initiation."

We were trying to think of some answers to give her when the waiter came up with the take-out box. Very carefully the ECKist put her half slice of cheesecake into the box and closed it. "What am I going to tell my friend when I get back about what it takes to get the Eighth Initiation?" she asked me again.

"Just tell her the answer is in the box," I said.

The Answer in the Box

When she got back, she said to her friend, "You know how you asked what it takes to get the Eighth Initiation?" "Yes, yes!" the friend answered eagerly. "The answer is in the box," the ECKist said.

Later I got a note from this friend. Apparently she had torn into the box, eaten the cheesecake, then sent this note that said, "I'm waiting."

It takes a great love for God to reach the higher worlds. Sometimes what brings you into the higher areas of spirituality is such a simple thing: first, being willing to share your piece of cheesecake. Being willing to share what you have.

I read in *Reader's Digest* that true generosity is not giving what you have but giving someone else what they need. This true generosity comes of true love.

Watching the Neighbors

If you live in a city, you have neighbors, and neighbors watch each other. I like to watch our neighbors.

The place next to ours is rental property, and people there come and go. The property has a peculiar monster called the long grass monster. This monster takes whoever tries to cut the grass and ties them up in weeds. Nobody could ever cut the grass over there until it became a crisis situation. Then the man who lived there would run outside with his lawnmower.

Anyone could tell he hated cutting that lawn.

The grass would be up to his ankles. He'd run up and down with his mower so fast that he'd snub the motor. He'd back up, and all these gobs of grass would come out. Then he'd start the mower again and go running off.

I told my wife, "Too bad he doesn't cut his grass more often. I so enjoy watching him." No matter what I was doing, I would always stop to watch him cut the grass.

Then he moved out, and a new couple moved in. The woman took charge of the lawn.

I have never seen a person attack a lawn like that. She didn't cut the grass once a month like the previous tenants; she attacked it twice a week. She cut the grass so short that it cried for mercy. I've never seen anyone who loved cutting grass as much as this woman.

After she cut the grass, she'd get out the blower and clean up. Then she'd back the car out of the garage and wash and polish it until it shone. I don't know what her mate was doing, but he was never out in the yard. The woman had so much energy.

These are the little things in life. If you love God, it's enough just to see what's going on around you and appreciate the show God has given you—sometimes in your own backyard.

World by the Bird Feeder

We watch the animals and birds that come to our backyard feeder too. They always fight.

A family of robins we raised a couple of years ago fight over the birdbath every morning. Dad gets to the birdbath first and just waits. Then Mom arrives; she's got to go off to work and find worms. She can't wait all morning for the birdbath. So they fight. Pretty soon they both go off to work, and the kids arrive. When they're all finished fighting, they fly away.

Next to arrive are the blackbirds and sparrows. Then the blue jays come and try to scare off the sparrows so they can fight with the blackbirds.

Just like people, I thought, *always fighting.* Then I noticed the three squirrels by the food dish on the ground. They're always fighting too.

Then comes the night crew, the three raccoons. They can get so fat. They eat the seed so fast they choke on it and cough. Then they begin fighting, and one of the raccoons tries to carry the food dish off. "You must be watching people," I told them.

Humans say to their kids, "Stop fighting like animals." I bet the animals say, "Stop fighting like people." Where else do animals and birds learn these things?

Enjoy Life Now

People worry about Judgment Day coming. But there's a need in humans to be greater than somebody else, to lord it over someone else, to take their seed away. When this need is out of people, that's when I think Judgment Day will come. When there's peace in every human heart. I don't think there's a reason for earth to end until people have worked out their problems.

Fear keeps us from enjoying life. In Christ's time, his disciples thought the last day would literally come. The early Christians believed it for a couple of hundred years. This is why there were so many martyrs—they had nothing to live for. "To die is gain," said Saint Paul.

All those centuries people worried about the last day, being afraid and wasting perfectly good lives. Why do that?

Live your own life, and try to live it with the love of God instead of with the fear of God. This is the message for these times, the message of truth for all times.

Try to live the love of God, because in so doing you will become a greater person. This is the only way to become a greater person.

Understanding the Law of Karma

Rules passed on to us by our parents, church leaders, and political leaders are not going to make us better spiritual beings. That is trying to impose outer rules on Soul, which works by an entirely different set of guidelines. Soul works by other rules—rules that sometimes the human consciousness isn't aware of.

One of these rules is: You pay for everything you get.

This is the Law of Karma. It makes sense, and you as Soul know this. You as a human being may not know this, and if you don't, it leads to irresponsible behavior. You may say, "I can do what I want and ask someone else for forgiveness, because at the last hour I will be saved. Someone else will lift this burden from me."

For what? Just for asking? It's not true; it's not the spiritual law.

You can kid yourself and live your life in this irresponsible way. But then you have no one else to blame for your troubles. It makes you a victim, a helpless victim of fate. Life steps on you. Well, whose fault is it? You may answer, "I don't know. It just happened." Troubles seem to come into your life out of the blue.

Beyond the Victim Consciousness

Soul is always in charge of Its own destiny.

This is why I'm trying to bring out the information that you are Soul. It lifts you from the material to the spiritual consciousness. Then it's just a matter of sticking with it and allowing this consciousness to grow in you— that you are Soul and you can do something about your life.

You can be an active instead of a passive person. You can take charge. You don't have to be the victim.

This doesn't mean life will be easier for you; it's often harder because, instead of sliding down the hill, you are making some effort to use your God-given talents to walk up. Life may get harder, but it will also get a lot richer. This is all I can promise you in ECK: a richer life.

Dream Message

In ECK we work with a dream teacher, the Dream Master. You can call it whatever you want. When you begin to accept the fact that you are Soul, you are opening yourself to a new level of spiritual understanding. In a year or two you may begin remembering your dreams. They may be very jumbled at first, and there will be a lot of symbolism to wade through. But stick with it.

The dream message that's coming to you in the human self—as you wake up in the morning and rub your eyes and wonder what the dream was all about—is from you, Soul, and the Mahanta, the inner side of the spiritual leader. He is the dream teacher, or Dream Master, giving you an experience in the other worlds. It goes through different layers of consciousness and gets scrambled as it reaches the human self.

But it's the higher self, Soul, trying to get a message through to you in the human form. Your higher part is trying to speak to your lower self to uplift you spiritually. To make you become more aware in this lifetime.

Wave of Love

You are becoming aware of why you even bother with living. And how to live better, how to live a more worthwhile life so that when the cycle finishes for you, you can say, "I have lived a good life, and I'm ready to go eagerly to see what lies in the other worlds." You will go with confidence and courage because you will be traveling on a wave of love.

And you will have found this wave of love in this lifetime. You can ride it during sleep into the inner worlds of God and there find the love, mercy, and peace that you have been looking for in this world but could never find.

A Great Love for God

An ECKist was reading her monthly discourses one evening. At the end I had written, "In contemplation, ask the Mahanta, 'What does "a great love for God" mean?' Then watch for the answer. It will come in either your outer life or your dreams, or both."

When the ECKist woke up the next morning, her dreams made no sense whatsoever. She tried to piece them together without success.

Her seven-year-old daughter was leaving for school just then. As she leaned down to kiss her daughter, she shut her eyes, thinking of the great love she had in her life. Her family and her two daughters were a great blessing to her.

In that moment, the little girl looked up and said, "Open your eyes, Mommy."

So the mother kissed her daughter with her eyes open, and they both laughed. In the next second the little girl ran out the door to school, and it hit the mother that she had gotten the answer to her question of the night before.

A great love for God means keeping your eyes open. The answer didn't come in the dream state; it came from her daughter. It was: Keep your eyes open, and see the love of God that is all around you.

Look for the love of God in your everyday life.

Find joy in the little things, places other people would never stoop to look, but you do because you know this is where God has hidden the secret of love. Love is not in high positions, or riches, or having the esteem of many people, or being a great public figure.

God has hidden the secret of love in the lowly places. And too many people are too vain to stoop down to look for it.

They're looking everywhere else—in the sky, in their wallets, in the electronics catalogs. But they can't find love, they can't find God, they can't find anything. They haven't bowed low enough to look for the love where God has put it. Love and awareness are in the most humble places. Look there.

May the blessings be.

ECK Worldwide Seminar, Minneapolis, Minnesota, Saturday, October 26, 1991

The man smiled just a little bit and said thank you back. Just an ordinary incident in the life of an average Soul, nothing big. But this feeling of love for God carried on throughout the day.

3

An Ordinary Day
in the Life of Soul

This is the Year of Light and Sound. The ECK, or Holy Spirit, manifests as Light and Sound. And this Light and Sound of God, the Voice of God, speaks to us in many ways—in our dreams and also in our daily lives.

Experiences of the Saints

The experiences people have in ECK are probably among the most esoteric experiences that are happening in a group of people today. Individuals throughout the centuries have had their visions of heaven; we call these people saints. In ECK, people are having these visions of heaven, but we're taking it a step further.

We're bringing these visions back to earth and using the knowledge and wisdom we gain from them in our daily lives. What kind of person do we try to become? We try to become more responsible for what we do.

If something goes wrong in our lives, we say, "Somehow, in some way, I was responsible for what happened."

We are a path of mystical experiences. When I say mystical, I am speaking in the sense of having a vision of heaven, of being able to go to the inner planes in our

29

dreams and sometimes more directly through Soul Travel. Soul Travel just means moving to a higher state of awareness and seeing what occurs on the inner planes.

Reality of Inner Worlds

Once you become familiar with the continuity of life, you find that the other worlds are actually very interesting places.

What we remember as dreams are usually broken memories of what really occurs there. The memories and facts are turned around, and we come out of the dream with fantastic remembrances of what took place. There are jumps in the experience where all of a sudden magic seems to occur.

And in some of these heavens things do occur that are beyond the laws of the physical universe. You find yourself able to fly. You're completely alive and aware in another state of experience, in a heaven.

In the past people who had such experiences had no one around to validate them. They often ended up in monasteries, contemplating in cells. They would have more and more of these experiences and become very out of touch with life here on earth. They became useless. Other monks would tend the garden, take care of the crops and the animals, and bring in food. But these people who had visions were unable to function as normal human beings who are responsible for themselves.

In ECKANKAR, there are some inner experiences you'll have to keep to yourself because people will not understand them if you talk about them. But at the same time, keep them in perspective. Know that others are having them too.

This is why these ECK seminars and the *ECKANKAR Journal* are so important.

The *ECKANKAR Journal* compiles stories of people who have had some connection with the Light and Sound, the Holy Spirit. Sometimes it's protection in accidents. Other times it's seeing the dream teacher, the Dream Master, and learning something from the experience about how to live their lives better.

An Ordinary Day in the Life of Soul

Someone wrote to me about a very ordinary day. As I read it, I said, "This is typical of what life in the love of God is like for people." It's something you really cannot explain. It is like a very special day, like your birthday when you were five years old.

This ECKist lives in Minneapolis. On this day he described, he had to go to the dentist early in the morning. Most of us would hear that and say, "This is not an ordinary day. And it's not something to look forward to." Generally it is pain that leads us to visit the dentist. Dentists have to be compassionate people to go into a profession like that where they fix up the problems people have made for themselves by wrong eating or habits of hygiene.

Trip to the Dentist

As this ECKist drove to his dental appointment, he said to himself, I'm going to fill myself with the love of God and just take things easy.

And as he drove into downtown, the traffic seemed to be slower that day. He found a parking lot and parked his car in the vicinity of the medical building. But he realized he didn't know exactly where the dentist's office was. He would have to ask somebody.

He got in the elevator to go to the skyway, a series of connecting passageways between the downtown buildings. In this elevator was a middle-aged businessman. As they were getting off, the businessman suddenly asked the ECKist, "Can I help you with where you're going?"

Maybe I look lost, the ECKist thought, but actually it was because he was so full of peace and love that day. "Yes, I need directions," he told the man.

The businessman directed him to the medical building, and as they parted, the ECKist gave the man a very warm and loving thank-you. He put himself behind it and really meant it.

Respect for Another Soul

His dental appointment went fine, and he walked back through the skyway to his car.

As he was driving out to pay the parking-lot cashier, he noticed the cashier looked like he was on skid row. He wore a rumpled fatigue shirt that looked unwashed. Maybe he slept in the streets at night but came to work at least often enough to buy whatever made him happy. But the ECKist looked at the man and thought, *This is another Soul. This Soul, for whatever reason, feels he has to wear these clothes and adopt that kind of attitude as defiance against the world.*

The cashier saw the look of respect in the ECKist's eyes for him as a human being, another Soul. He handed the ECKist his change, and the ECKist said, "Thank you," not overdoing it but meaning it from his heart. And the man smiled just a little bit and said thank you back.

Just an ordinary incident in the life of an average Soul, nothing big. But this feeling of love for God carried on throughout the day.

You Have Made Your World

The love of God is in the very smallest things, the most private experiences of your life.

They don't have to be these great inner flights of Soul, the great dream experiences, although they may be. Accept life as you find it around you, because this is the world you have made from your understanding of what God and the Holy Spirit are.

If it's a world of mystery, if it's a harsh or cruel world, you have made it so through you own lack of understanding of what God is.

There are some people who are happy under the most severe conditions and physical hardships you can imagine. They are happy even when they have no food, no shelter. Yet in our affluent society there are people who are unhappy although they can have anything they want. With every material thing in hand, they blame others for what they don't have. Probably it's because they haven't yet shown gratitude for what God has given them.

Ungrateful people can never be happy. They can never be generous because their world begins and ends within themselves. It's a totally self-centered world. To grow spiritually you have to somehow get to be a person with your attention on God, on love. Then you'll find the great things in the little things.

Don't be afraid to stoop low to look for the love that God has placed around you, because it's there. If you're not finding it, it's probably because you're too proud to stoop low enough to look for it.

A Cat Named Scrap

I got a letter from one of our friends in England. She's an elderly woman. She had a cat named Scrap that she had to have put to sleep. This was a very great loss for her. Our pets become our very close friends; when they leave there is a great emptiness in our lives, and we don't know if we'll ever get another pet.

During one of this woman's empty days, she looked out her window into the garden and saw a little black kitten. Somehow it had jumped over the six-foot fence into the backyard. The woman said, "I don't want to start feeding this kitten. It probably belongs to someone else, and it should go home."

But she put food out because the kitten was very hungry.

This woman has a way with cats, and as time went on the kitten appeared every morning, waiting for her breakfast. This concerned the woman, but she'd put the food out anyway. Months went by, and one morning she noticed the young cat was pregnant.

The woman ended up as midwife with five more kittens in her house.

Love Conquers Loneliness

With five kittens in her care, the woman no longer had the freedom to travel to seminars or to see friends and family as often. But then she noticed that the mother cat began to take on some of the characteristics of her old friend Scrap. She started to wonder if the young cat was Scrap come back in a new body. So she decided to keep the cat and some of the kittens.

She had wanted her freedom to travel, but life is day

to day. And it can get very lonely. She realized that, for now, no matter what happens to her, God has given her someone to love and need her.

We need to be needed in life.

If there is no more purpose, no one to depend on us, then we've actually outlived our usefulness. If there's some way we can be of help and service to others, that means we still have a reason to live.

This cat, which at first was an extra burden, became a way for the woman to give and get love.

Life Becomes Richer, Not Easier

Someone asked me, "Why do I feel such pain? I'm in ECK, and I feel the pain of separation more than I felt it before. Why after all this time is this pain so much stronger?"

And I answered, "The more the love, the more the pain."

I'm not promising that you'll have an easier life in ECK. In fact, in many ways it'll be more difficult. But it will be a rich life. And you will learn to love.

Even as you learn to love more, you will feel the pain of life more because you're becoming more sensitive to the love of God. You're understanding more of how people feel when they are going through their hard times.

What would be easier? To become more unconscious, to not notice when someone hurts. This would make life very easy for you, but you wouldn't be much more than a rock. And this isn't the purpose of Soul.

You, as an individual, are to become more aware of God's love. What makes you aware of this love?

The experiences you have in your daily life.

And the experiences that teach you about love are often those of pain. Pain teaches God's love. We don't like pain, we don't like change, but they are blessings in disguise. They teach us to become more godlike.

People say, "ECKANKAR doesn't promise me an easy road to heaven. It doesn't say that no matter what I do, I'll be forgiven. It gives me responsibility for what I do, promising me more love but also the greater pain of knowing what greater love is. I don't know if I can handle that."

Much of the teaching in ECK comes inwardly. It comes through your dreams, through your insight and intuition about what's happening in your life every day. ECKANKAR is an inner and outer teaching. This is what gives it the dynamic that it has.

Punctuality

Someone asked me if I'd say a word about punctuality. I used to be very punctual. But sometimes you find the people around you aren't.

The problem about being on time is that you have to wait for the people who aren't. If a meeting is scheduled to start at a certain time, just start at that time. Don't wait for latecomers; just go ahead.

If you're meeting with one other person and the person is late, you're going to have to wait. That's how it is.

The Special Dress

An ECKist arrived a few days early for an ECK seminar in Anaheim, California, this past summer. She decided to go shopping and took a shuttle bus to a nearby mall with a friend. In a dress shop in the mall, the woman saw the most beautiful dress, but it was very expensive, way beyond anything she'd ever spent before on a dress.

The dress was everything she wanted, but it was one size too big.

The salesperson said, "We can get you the right size from our store in Los Angeles. It will only take a day or two. We'll have it here by Sunday afternoon." The woman said, "Great."

The ECK seminar was over Sunday morning, and the woman packed her bags and took the shuttle bus back to the mall. But the dress was nowhere to be found. The salesperson looked all over the shop for it and finally said, "I think we sent it back to Los Angeles by mistake." The ECKist was heartbroken.

Is there a way I can take the size larger dress and pull the drawstrings tighter? she wondered.

As she was trying it on, she noticed a very attractive woman with long, dark hair. The woman was trying on a dress about three times more expensive than the ECKist's dress. "That's a very beautiful dress," she couldn't help but say to the young woman.

The young woman smiled and thanked her. Then the two went back to their own dresses, both trying to make a decision.

At that moment, the salesperson came over. "I found the dress in your size at another store in this area. But you'll have to go get it. There's nobody here who has a car." The ECKist only had the shuttle bus. "I guess I can't," she said. "My plane leaves this afternoon, so I can't come back tomorrow for it."

Two New Friends

An elderly woman in the back of the store spoke up. "If you really want to go to that store, my daughter and I will take you," she said to the ECKist.

37

It turned out that the elderly woman and young woman with the dark hair were mother and daughter.

"Do you really mean it?" said the ECKist. "Yes, we mean it. If you want the dress, we'll take you to get it if you don't mind spending the afternoon on our shopping trip with us."

This ECKist had been feeling very lonely throughout the seminar. A number of her friends were all going to stop off at Las Vegas on the way home to have a good time. Because she had to work the next day she couldn't go with them, although she wanted to very much. She had been feeling very low when she walked into the dress shop.

But here she had bumped into this kind woman and her daughter. They all got into the woman's car and continued on the shopping trip.

On the way, the ECKist began to find out about the two people. Despite the expensive dress the young woman had purchased, the family wasn't at all wealthy. The husband was in construction; they had an average home in the hills surrounded by beautiful mansions. The daughter was buying the expensive dress to attend the tenth-year reunion of her high school class. She had been very heavy when she was in school.

"My daughter's so slim now, she would like a dress to feel good in when she sees her former classmates. They won't recognize her," the mother told the ECKist. "Even though the dress is costing us a lot, it's worth every penny."

The ECKist could see that the mother simply loved her family. Money at this time was no object.

They stopped at the store, and the ECKist bought her dress. Then the mother and daughter invited her to stay for dinner, but she had to catch her flight home. As they were dropping her at the shuttle bus to go back to her hotel, her two new friends said, "If you're ever in town again, please stop by. There are other shops we want to show you."

Love Is Love

The ECKist was able to wear this very special dress to a wedding that was held at the Temple of ECK this year. The dress will always be special for her because she found it when she was most lonely, when she was feeling the pain of separation from her friends at the ECK seminar. But if you follow where life leads you, God will show you how to make your life better. God will show you love, and this woman found it.

She knows it's a dress of love. Of course, love is not in a material thing. Love just is love. But sometimes when you have something like this dress that you bought with friends, you will always have this glow of love when you wear such a special garment.

On your journey home, my love is always with you. And we'll keep the light on for you.

ECK Worldwide Seminar, Minneapolis, Minnesota,
Sunday, October 27, 1991

Take care of what needs to be done when the sun shines so that you can sleep when the night comes and the wind begins to blow.

4

I Can Sleep When the Wind Blows

No matter how advanced people claim they are, when it gets right down to it, very few people like change.

Glasses

On my first visit to Australia in 1981, people were upset that I wore glasses in my position as the Living ECK Master. Two years later I got contact lenses. Then new people who came into ECK would find out I used to wear glasses and what seemed to be natural eyesight wasn't. They thought this was a trick of science. But I told them, "I'm just trying to see you. It's one of those things."

Here I am back in glasses today because my eye doctor goofed. I've come full circle—from glasses to contacts to glasses again.

ECK-Vidya Speaks

It happened in a curious way. I've been going to an eye doctor who likes the new technology; he likes to find out what's new on the market. Then he tries to fit me, and everything goes wrong.

One time I was waiting at the doctor's office, and an elderly woman came out of the back. Her husband was sitting next to me. "Did you get your new glasses?" he asked. "No, he goofed up," she said.

She looked directly at me when she said it.

This is the ECK, Divine Spirit, giving me the ECK-Vidya, the ancient science of prophecy, I thought. It's Divine Spirit's way of telling me that my prescription is going to be goofed up too. Sure enough, the doctor came out and told me.

"We'll order another lens," he reassured me, and he told me to come back in two weeks, right before I left on this trip.

Two weeks later I went in, only to find out that the prescription was goofed up again. He's a good doctor, but he let one of his assistants do the work. One of them wrote up my prescription for the wrong eye. The doctor did a lot of apologizing.

Seeing Life Clearly

The spiritual path is about seeing. It's about seeing life. How we see life affects how we live life. So to live life correctly, you have to see life correctly.

When I was younger, back in school, I used to have very good vision. I went to school in the city and visited back home on the farm. During one visit I was in the woods, and all of a sudden I found it was very hard to focus on the trees. Some were fuzzy. I couldn't understand this because they used to be so clear. For two years I couldn't admit to myself that I couldn't see well.

Our class at school was divided into three sections, seated alphabetically. *Klemp* fell at the end of the first section, so I was always seated in the back row. I missed a lot of what was going on at the front of the room on the blackboard.

When we had a multiple-choice test, I'd study the odds. Twenty-five questions, four choices for each—that's one hundred chances to be wrong. So I studied all the different ways you could take a test without knowing any of the material. Such as, how many times could choice *a* be the right choice? It was random selection.

This sort of selection process put me at odds with the teacher. He figured knowledge was of one sort; I realized it depended on how you saw things. And from the back of the room, I wasn't seeing too much of anything he put on the board. In biology class, he came up with all these incredible Latin names that I couldn't remember, so I had to make things up when I took the test. For a while there, I almost flunked out.

Correcting Your Vision

As you do in life sometimes when you can't see clearly, you don't do so well. And what was the reason back then?

I wouldn't admit to myself or anyone else that I couldn't see. I reached a point where I knew I was going to have to do some serious studying to stay in school. It became a matter of pride versus shame, which gave me the incentive.

So I got glasses, and I was very embarrassed.

The next visit back home, I was very aware that everyone knew I had glasses. I was sure that the kids would tell me, "You look awful in those things. Sure hope you can see better than you look." But when I stood around with everyone after church, one of my friends finally asked me, "Did you just get those glasses or did you have them in grade school?"

Suddenly I got the feeling that people weren't noticing the glasses as much as I thought. People I'd gone to school with for seven years didn't know whether or not I'd had them when I left for boarding school.

If we can see clearly in life, if we have the right spiritual vision, then we ought to be able to do something well in our lives.

What Would Make You Happy?

There are so many people who are unhappy with their lives. They're unhappy at work, unhappy with their families, and even unhappy on their vacations. It's because what they expect from life is quite different from what they're getting. There is a gap. I often wonder if it's because what they expect is unrealistic or if their lives are unrealistic.

Most people live a life of illusion. There is a gap between their hopes and how their lives are actually turning out.

Some people have an idea that if they won a sweepstakes, they would be so happy. Other people feel they would be very happy if they had good health. Some people have very serious, life-threatening conditions.

I met one such person who had had an organ transplant. "You look really well," I said. "Your color's back. How are things going?"

"Still problems," she said.

"With your health?" I asked. "No, other things," she said. "My marriage now."

Being Needed

She had found out that until her operation her marriage had been based on the fact that she was an invalid, that her husband was needed. He could take care of her.

He might have complained, and because he complained, she finally figured it was better to get the organ transplant. But she didn't realize that maybe what her husband needed most of all was to be needed.

When she had the operation, suddenly she could get a job, go to school, take courses in the medical field—things that would fulfill her in a way she had never had a chance to experience.

Suddenly she was an independent woman. She no longer depended on her husband as she had before. When the dependency was gone, the marriage began to falter. The couple had to look at their relationship in a new light. It meant putting on a new pair of glasses, looking at things in a way they had never done before.

A Mirror for the Self

So often we feel that if circumstances outside ourselves could change, we would be happy.

This is backward. We assume we are seeing truly, that if anything is wrong with our world it is the fault of something or someone outside ourselves.

If something goes wrong at work, it's because of a certain person there that we just can't stand. The assumption we carry is that whatever we see, whatever we feel is correct. And don't ever let anyone suggest that we're not seeing truly, that perhaps we're seeing through the eyes of illusion. That perhaps we need a new prescription for our glasses so that we could see spiritually.

If we could see spiritually, we might notice that our glasses are mirrors. We are expecting to look out, but instead we look in. Then we realize, *That's why everything is going wrong. The thinking inside me was wrong. My perception of life was wrong.*

A lot of people may look at a clock and say it's broken, it doesn't run. You set the alarm and it doesn't go off. You hold it to your ear and it doesn't make whirring noises. If it's an old windup clock, it doesn't go tick, tick. So we say it's broken. But maybe, maybe there's something wrong with how we look at life.

Maybe it's us. Maybe it's our spiritual hearing. Maybe the clock is working but we didn't hear the alarm go off.

I'm speaking here of seeing, and I'm speaking here of hearing. These are the two aspects of God, the Light and Sound. You see because of the Light. You hear because of the Sound. And these are the two aspects of God, or of the Holy Spirit.

The Holy Spirit actually is the Voice of God.

Experiences of Light and Sound

God and the Holy Spirit are not the same. Christianity runs around in a circle. I learned in church as a youth that God is the Holy Spirit, that Jesus is God, that God is not the Holy Spirit, and that Jesus is not God. It was very confusing. I couldn't ever make heads or tails of it.

Basically, there is God and there is the Holy Spirit. The Holy Spirit is the Voice of God. It is this Voice of God that we can hear as different sounds. Sometimes they are like the sounds of nature.

For instance, if you sit down quietly in contemplation or in prayer, you'll occasionally have the experience of hearing something like thunder. You think it's raining. You open your eyes, look out the window, and see the sun is shining. *That's strange,* you think, *I know I heard thunder.*

So you lay back on your bed, shut your eyes, and hear thunder again.

I mention this because people don't know what to think of it. The sky is perfectly clear. It's not any phenomenon such as the ground shifting. Sometimes it's simple: the person is hearing a sound of God. Notice that I said, "A sound of God." The Holy Spirit manifests Itself through a number of different sounds, such as running water or a sharp drumbeat.

It's almost like a drum that armies used to set the cadence for the troops marching. Sometimes in Africa we've heard it too; it almost sounds like people communicating with tom-toms. It's another sound of the Holy Spirit.

Messenger from God

Sometimes God speaks to us through a messenger. It's an inner being, one of the Masters or an angel.

Someone gives us a message; and if the messenger happens to have long hair and a glorified presence, the person immediately ties it in with a spiritual figure from his religious path. It's natural. Why? It's an experience that's out of the ordinary, and the person will reach for some connection with the highest spiritual personage he can think of.

He says, "I've had a visit by Jesus. Jesus talked to me." Or it'll be a saint that talked to him, depending on his beliefs. And often he becomes the leader of his path.

Sometimes the messenger will come in the dream state. Sometimes in the dream state the Mahanta, the inner side of myself, will come to people and tell them something they need to know about how to see better spiritually. They are having a problem in life. It has brought them to the very edge, and they wonder if they can take one more step, last one more day.

47

People on the Edge of Life

The people who look hardest for truth are those who are brought to the edge of despair. The rest of the people don't need truth. They have health, they have microwave ovens, they have a new car, they have all the conveniences that life can give. What do they need God for? There's plenty of time for God later, when they're on their deathbeds.

This is one of the biggest traps of society: modern conveniences make life so pleasant. Science has become our religion.

A long time ago, in the seventeenth century, the Irish prelate Ussher was doing studies about the knowledge that humankind had gathered up to that time. He took any writing that had ever been done and he tried to piece it all together.

He came up with what he thought was the age of the earth. He set the beginning of creation at 4004 B.C. He was using the knowledge he had in those days, trying to put it all together.

Matching Expectations and Reality

When your life is right, when you can see correctly, when you are seeing life without illusion and seeing yourself in relationship with life as it truly is—I think you will then be a truly happy person.

Why? Because when you see truly, then your hopes about what you expect in life are going to be very close to what you are getting out of life.

There's nothing wrong with dreaming big dreams or setting your sights high. The mistake comes when we expect that God is going to let us win the Reader's Digest sweepstakes and in the meantime we sit around waiting for the phone call. People wait and wait for fortune to fall on them. It's a passive way of living. I can almost assure you that this person will have about one chance in three hundred million to be happy.

Start where you are, begin with what you have.

Ask, "Where am I today? How can I build my own life with the help of the ECK?" Look at yourself squarely and say, "I am at this point today; where do I want to be in five years?"

There's nothing wrong with material things. The old saying in the Bible that people got wrong was "Money is the root of all evil." It's not money, it's the love of money. There's nothing wrong with a good car, a good television set, and a good home. These are all things we can rightly aspire to in this lifetime.

I Can Sleep When the Wind Blows

A farmer was looking for a hired hand. He put out classified ads and finally got a response from a young man.

"Can you bale hay?" the farmer asked him. The young man said, "No." "Do you know how to plow fields?" the farmer asked. "No," said the young man. "Do you know how to fix farm equipment?" "No," said the young man.

What kind of a person would come here and not know how to do anything? the farmer wondered to himself. "Well, what can you do?" he finally asked the young man.

"I can sleep when the wind blows," the young man said.

The farmer thought this was the strangest thing he'd ever heard, but after a few days when no one else came to apply for the job, he called up the young man. "You look strong and willing, so we'll give you a try," he said. And so the young man was hired on as the farmer's helper.

He learned very quickly. Before too long, he was a real asset to the farm.

One night a very bad storm hit. The farmer had turned a lot of his duties over to his hired man, and he had no idea where anything was anymore. Quickly, he ran upstairs to the hired man's room and tried to wake him. He shook the man's shoulders. "Hurry! There's a storm coming, and we've got to get the hay wagon inside the barn and secure everything. The wind's going to be bad." But the hired hand just grumbled a few times and kept on sleeping.

The farmer got really upset. He shook the man as hard as he could. "What's the matter with you? Don't you know a storm's coming? We've got to close the barn doors and get the hay wagon in." But the hired man just kept on sleeping.

At this point the farmer gave up. "Forget it," he said, disgusted, and ran outside into the night with the storm blowing around him. He found that the hay wagon was already inside the barn. The barn doors were already shut, and the big door to the barnyard was also closed.

Then the farmer realized what the young man had meant when he said, "I can sleep when the wind blows."

The young man had taken care of everything that needed taking care of. Because the young man could see truly, he knew what was important. He knew that if you're a farmer, you take care of what needs to be done when the sun shines so that you can sleep when the night comes and the wind begins to blow.

How to Fix Your Life

I'm offering you this challenge too. Take care of those things that you need to do to make your own life work.

You may be saying now, "OK, he's told us what's broken. But is he going to tell us how to fix it?"

Anyone can tell you what's broken. All I can offer you is the word *HU*. This is a name for God. Sing it to yourself, but first fill your heart with love.

When you're having any kind of trouble and you want an insight into what you can do or an understanding to get through the problem, sing the song of HU. It has the power of God, and it has the love of God in it. It's a beautiful song. It's the only gift I have to give you.

ECK South Pacific Regional Seminar, Sydney, Australia,
Saturday, November 23, 1991

51

Sit down and determine what you would like to have in your life. Make a reasonable plan to reach it. Then remember to sing HU, the love song to God.

5

The Law of Plenty

I was reading an article in a writer's magazine. The article said that writers have to first understand what their audience is there for. Why are they reading what you've written? I think this goes for speakers too. Why do people come to hear you?

You must first ascertain the audience's need. Did they come to laugh? Did they come to get information? Did they come for knowledge or wisdom or whatever? Before you finish the writing or finish your talk, you have to fulfill that need. Sometimes I feel I've succeeded and other times not.

When they pick up a newspaper or turn on the TV, people are always asking, "What's in it for me?"

The reason we ask this question is that so often we feel life doesn't give us enough. We're always looking for how life can give us more.

Making Things Happen

One of the best things we can hope for in life is to find spiritual freedom.

But a lot of people don't look for it. They never consider that they don't have freedom. They just figure that life is

53

life, that whatever happens in this lifetime happens. They don't worry about the hereafter.

They go through life pretty much as passive people. Things happen to them; they hardly ever make things happen. This, I feel, is the difference between the teachings of ECK and some other paths.

You can't put all the people on one side of this line or the other. Some people, no matter what religious teaching they follow, are active and make things happen. Other people let things happen to them, no matter what religion they follow. You've got one group of people that are mostly happy and another group who mostly aren't happy.

It's very difficult to get passive people to see that their lives are what they've made them.

It isn't that someone else sat on them or did something to them. In some way, through their attitude or deeds, they have created their own life.

This is one of the hardest things for people to accept, especially when I come onstage and tell them they are responsible for their own lives. Then they get upset with me. They don't want to know that they're responsible for what they've done, for what their life is. They want me to figure an easy way out of it. I wish I could, but I can't.

Plenty of Vision

I was talking with one of the RESAs before I came onstage. "We have six hundred people here tonight," he told me. "That is more than last time," I said. "Every year the number inches up." "I'm tired of inching," he said. "Next year I want three thousand."

He's one of those people who makes things happen. He has plenty of vision.

A First Step to Freedom

What does ECK offer people? It offers self-responsibility.

You say, "Self-responsibility? Gee, thanks. Life's hard enough." But ECK also offers spiritual freedom. I don't know if there's a way to get spiritual freedom unless you first develop self-responsibility.

How do you do that? By putting your attention on God in the right way.

One example I've given you is the song of HU.

When you sing HU, you are spiritualizing your attention. You are saying, "I am putting all my attention, heart, and Soul upon the highest good that I can imagine" instead of saying, "God, I'm having such a hard life, please help me out of this or that."

Sometimes we ask almost with the sense that there isn't enough to go around. We think the reason we are short of something in our life—the reason we lack things—is because there isn't enough to go around. We know God is good, but we think maybe God doesn't see us because we are just one little human being. Of course, when we have pain come into our life, all of a sudden we are very big.

For example, you have thirty-two teeth in your mouth, and you don't really notice them until you get a cavity. It starts to hurt. The pain in one tooth can feel like your whole head is hurting. It feels huge because it hurts so much.

What Is Important to You?

These are things we worry about. We age, and all of a sudden our bodies aren't able to run as fast. Things don't work as well.

Age creeping up becomes a source of fear. It reminds me of the old song, "I'll Never Get Out of This World Alive." So you wonder, *What are we here for? Just to be passive, to put in our time? That seems like a sheep's way to live. I'd like to be more active. I would like to have at least a few things in this life go my way.*

Sometimes material things are a stumbling block for a person on the path to God. This is simply because people look at material things in the wrong way.

There's nothing wrong with having the good things of life for ourselves or our family. Sometimes we don't necessarily care to make this a life of prosperity because other things are more important to us—family, the good opinion of others, love.

Plenty of Protection

One of the members of ECKANKAR's Board of Trustees was flying to a meeting in Minneapolis from the East Coast. When he got on the plane, he noticed it was Flight 13. "Doesn't look good," the man said to himself.

The flight stopped in Chicago to take on passengers and continued on to Minneapolis. As the plane approached the Minneapolis airport, a heavy fog rolled in. It closed the airport. The plane circled Minneapolis for a while along with all the other circling planes. The man knew his fellow board members were probably circling up there too.

Finally the air traffic controller sent the plane back to Chicago. The passengers waited there for a while, until the fog seemed to clear in Minneapolis. Then the plane took off again. But as soon as they approached the Minneapolis airport, the fog rolled in again and shut them out.

So air traffic control sent them back to Chicago again.

It looked like the passengers would have to spend the

night there. Finally the airport authorities said they'd send the plane one more time, and this time they were able to land.

When the ECKist got on the ground, he calculated his travel time. A flight that was normally three hours long had taken thirteen. When he checked into the hotel where the board members were staying, he realized they were on the thirteenth floor.

In a case like this you have to say: plenty of protection.

It doesn't mean we always get through, but so what? We live in the light and love of the Holy Spirit, the ECK. We go through life loving the Holy Spirit, loving God, and loving life. And if we can do this, we've done a lot.

Taking Initiative with Soul Travel

As the teacher on this path, I've found that people often come to ECK and want to get out of the body because they want to get away from the life they've made for themselves. A lot of times, it's a mess. I can see why they would just want to get away from it. But an attitude like this actually is saying: "I'm just going to forget about this lifetime and wait for heaven, because heaven has got to be better." They take no action to begin creating heaven here and now.

Why do they wait? Because they think that change is something that has to be done outside of their skin. They want to go where things are pretty; they want to Soul Travel.

Soul Travel does give a person happy experiences a lot of the time. It depends where you go. But at least if you want to do Soul Travel, it shows you are willing to take the initiative in something. You're willing to be the cause. That's why it's one of the aspects of ECK.

For people who haven't had the courage to take charge of their lives out here, they can start spiritually. They can try to take charge of their lives inwardly. Once they start inwardly, it can then work outwardly.

Changes begin within you, not out here.

Spiritual Learning

This is why ECK is an inner teaching. Much of the teaching I do is through your dreams. I find people are more open this way.

Out here, we have ideas of how we will fail—and sure enough, we build a whole life to prove it. We have surrounded ourselves with failure and the lack of plenty. Even our requests of life and of God are made with reservations: "Please, God, if you can."

What do you mean—if you can?

All the power of the universes is in the Creator's hand. If something is for your spiritual good, it would work out for you instantly. But so often it isn't for your spiritual good.

Why not? Because you haven't learned something spiritually that you need to know.

Why do you have to know anything spiritually? Why do you have to improve spiritually? Well, if you're going to go to heaven and just sit there enjoying life, of course you don't need to improve in any way. But in ECK, you begin in this life to learn to become a Co-worker with God. This is your destiny—not just to go to heaven and enjoy yourself. Anybody can do that.

This doesn't mean that if you're choosing to become a Co-worker with God that you cannot enjoy life, beginning right here. You're learning to take charge of things. There is no feeling quite as satisfying as knowing that you have accomplished some little goal in your own life.

Start with a Reasonable Plan

Begin to accomplish the little goals here. How do you do that? You make a plan.

If you want a new car, make a plan. Don't leave it up to God, the Creator with the infinite power who could make you a car almost as an afterthought. If God wanted to let you win the Reader's Digest sweepstakes, you would very easily. People ask, "If I pray to God and ask for this, why don't I get it?" God looks down and says, "Because you haven't learned anything yet."

You're not necessarily here to have a good life. You're here to grow spiritually. And until you grow spiritually, you're not going to get the good things you want.

One way to grow and get things in this life is to take responsibility and make a plan. And it has to be a reasonable plan. It has to be something within the range of your talents and skills. You have to start where you are. You can't say, "By next week I plan to increase my income ten times." It's not going to work, because if you had that skill you would already have that increase right now. But you don't, so it means you haven't developed that skill. So set up a reasonable plan, maybe to reach that ten times increase in ten different steps. Break the plan into ten steps, and try to do a little bit at a time.

You start somewhere; you make a plan. Then you say, "I've done my best. Now I put it into the hands of Divine Spirit." You keep yourself open constantly to whatever guidance the ECK is giving you to help you achieve your goal, if this is the goal that is going to help you grow spiritually.

59

Overcoming Your Limitations

You have to realize that you are starting as a limited human being suddenly set down in a world of plenty. There is no limitation except for the limitations you have made for yourself. These limitations are very real. You're not going to overcome them in a week.

One way to begin coming into a greater vision of life is to sing HU when you need help. You say, "I've made my plan. I'm now asking for God's help." Then as you work toward your plan, remember to sing HU.

Things won't always go the way you plan. That's when you have to go back and make contact with the Divine Force.

Minute-by-Minute Guidance

A student from New Zealand had come into ECK a few years ago. He liked the idea of Soul Travel; he wanted to get out of the body. This is what drew him to ECKANKAR. But along the way he lost any inclination for Soul Travel. Rather, he lives his life now along the lines of *The Book of ECK Parables,* where you try to find answers from the Holy Spirit in the small, minute-by-minute happenings of your daily life.

This is how the Holy Spirit will work with you. It will give you a little instruction here, a little there.

Sometimes it isn't an instruction; the Holy Spirit will send a person to help you. Sometimes you miss the help because you're looking too far away. You're looking ten rows back, and the person is right in front of you.

Sometimes you have to take the smallest step, just to gain momentum to take another step, then another. Set

60

your goal small enough so that you can win, so that you can achieve something. As you gain the small step, as you gain more momentum, you're going to gain confidence in your ability to do something with your life. This is how you go about it. And then you'll find you have plenty of divine love.

Proof of Protection

One night the ECKist from New Zealand said, "I know I have the love and protection of the Holy Spirit, but it would be good to have proof." He wasn't remembering his dreams; he wasn't having any of the sensational experiences you'd normally associate with a path like ours.

He's a tai chi chuan instructor, and at one of his classes soon after this he was helping a student with a move. Suddenly she leaned close to him and said, "I hope you don't think I'm crazy but all through this class session I've been seeing two men standing behind you. One is in a deep red robe; he might be Tibetan. The other is an older man with a white beard. There's an incredible amount of love coming from both of them."

Right away the ECKist knew these were the ECK Masters Rebazar Tarzs and Fubbi Quantz. His request for proof was answered. He was moving forward spiritually. And this help came not only to him but as a benefit to another person too.

This woman in his class didn't know about ECKANKAR or the ECK Masters. But the experience touched her and came to him secondhand. He never saw that student in his classes again.

This is the reality of the ECK teachings. We have a real path, and it's up to you to find the reality and love in it.

61

Law of Plenty

A group of ECKists were giving a workshop at the ECK Worldwide Seminar on donations to ECKANKAR. They were wondering how to go about it. They felt people were tired of being asked for donations for the ECK missions. So one of the facilitators suggested, "We could talk about the law of prosperity."

This viewpoint says that there's enough for everybody. This is the creation of plenty. There is more than enough if people just know how to find the blessings of God.

So they were talking back and forth about the law of prosperity as they gave their workshop, and they began to talk about people who give larger and larger donations to ECK. They forgot to talk about everybody else.

One of the people in the group who had devoted his life to serving ECK got very upset. "What you forget," he said, "is that not everyone has come into this life to be rich. There are some people who come here to raise families because that is what they want. Wealth doesn't mean anything to them beyond providing enough for their families to grow up and have opportunities, such as an education, proper clothing, and food. This is all these people care about."

"There are other people," he continued, "who just care enough about prosperity to be able to teach for ECKANKAR. They don't want to be rich. When you're onstage talking about the law of prosperity, they don't relate to what you are saying."

"What about me?" he said. "I don't have a lot to give. But I always give a little. I give what I can because to me, wealth is what I give to life. Then life gives it back to me."

Other Kinds of Riches

This person had a good perspective on the Law of Plenty. He felt he was rich because he had a loving mate, loving children, and a good home. He was rich in a way that probably no one else on earth would understand. Sometimes people who consider themselves rich don't have a home but they have friends. They say, "I am happy here, and I am growing spiritually." I think these are the people who are living according to the Law of Plenty.

They have found the richness of the Holy Spirit within them. And because they have, they are the ones who go out into the world and give much more than wealth to the people they meet every day. They may give donations to ECKANKAR, whatever they can. But they also give divine love. This is the greatest gift of all.

If you want spiritual freedom, you have to give freedom to others.

If you want something from life, you first have to give to life in some way. You may choose to give donations, but more important, choose to give to others.

Key of Gratitude

Give to others not just what you have, but what they need. There's a difference. True generosity is giving to others what they need.

If you want to bring more of the blessings of God into your life, first of all sit down and determine what you would like to have in your life. You have to know that first. Then make a reasonable plan to reach it. Then remember to sing HU, the love song to God.

Go about your life with love and thanksgiving. If you can do that, I think you will find that the Law of Plenty

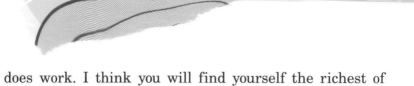

does work. I think you will find yourself the richest of people. May the blessings be.

South Pacific Regional Seminar, Sydney, Australia,
Sunday, November 24, 1991

Once you can recognize the spiritual community you are part of, then you will recognize that you are worshiping whenever you treat other people with respect, as divine beings, as Soul.

6

The Spiritual Community

Every so often I hear someone say, "We've got to get the ECK community together." But I want to talk about the spiritual community.

The spiritual community is actually larger. It includes all groups that most of us take for granted, and it includes all religions.

What Is a Spiritual Community?

A spiritual community includes the Christians, the Jews, the Hindus, the Muslims, and all the other religions. It includes them all. And within each of these groups exists not just one spiritual community, but many.

There are spiritual communities of many different sizes—from small to immense—all around us. And within these communities, people are becoming more pure and uplifted individuals.

So often we feel that when we worship, we should worship on the Sabbath. But what do we do the rest of the week? Sometimes people might stretch prayer to include worship, but most don't actually think of prayer as worship.

There's a British sitcom called *Are You Being Served?*
It shows what a spiritual community is. To define a spiritual community, it is any group of three or more people
who are of a common purpose and like mind, who are
growing spiritually but usually don't know it.

Spiritual Service

Most people are not aware that they are part of a
spiritual community, but the community exists whether
people are conscious of it or not. What service does it
offer? What does it do?

It lets people bump into each other and work out their
problems with each other.

A family is a community. In the family, people have
problems. There's a hierarchy—there are the parents who
are in charge. Then there are the kids who feel they are
the slaves or servants. This goes on until there's a shift of
power, probably when the child becomes a teenager. Then
for a while nobody's really sure who runs the show.

Cartoons are a good example of how people interact
with each other, how they solve problems with each other.
At the end of it, they've changed, hopefully for the better.
There are also more dramatic television shows such as *I'll
Fly Away* or *Northern Exposure*. But they are a little bit
involved. That's why I chose *Are You Being Served?* for our
purpose today.

The Problem of Listening

One of the biggest problems in a community—whether
it's a family, at work, or a social club—is listening. People
do not listen to each other. Problems arise when someone
speaks and others do not understand.

Problems also arise when someone doesn't live up to another person's expectations.

For instance, a parent tells the child, "Clean your room." A little while later the child appears in the kitchen wanting a cookie. "Room clean?" asks the parent. "Yes," says the child. "Can I have a cookie now?" "First I'm going to check your room," says the parent.

When the parent goes into the child's room, it looks as bad as before. A few things are rearranged, but the parent thinks nothing's changed. The child thinks he has just made a massive cleanup of the room. What's happened here?

Miscommunication. The parent is seeing things one way, and the child sees something entirely different. So they have a problem.

What Conflict Brings

In a spiritual community you'll always find a complication or a problem. In a television show, it's the basis of comedy or of drama. It's the basis of movies and stories.

When the problem occurs, the community is tested. Is the community going to be strong enough? Is each individual going to be strong enough to say, I will do the right thing? Or will one person bend to the outer pressure that threatens to destroy the community?

There is a wealth of information of a spiritual nature in shows like this. I want you to get an idea of what it means to be a member of a spiritual community.

When a child goes to school each day, he leaves the spiritual community of home to enter the community of the classroom. But maybe he hasn't finished a report that's due. The teacher says, "John, where's your report?" The child says, "The dog ate it." "That's too bad," says the

69

teacher. "You know I can't accept that." So the problem occurs as the child leaves one spiritual community and enters another. The child hasn't done his homework, and there's going to be a problem.

How do you get out of this? A lot of times you don't; you just have to take it. On sitcoms, they usually resolve the problem by the end of the show, and things are different than when the show started.

Are You Being Served?

Are You Being Served? takes place in a store in England, Grace Brothers, mostly in the men's and women's apparel departments. Captain Peacock is the floorwalker; his name fits him because he's like a peacock. He doesn't do much except look good, and the symbol of his authority is the red carnation on his lapel. A customer comes in and he asks them, "May I help you?" then directs them to the right department. It doesn't look like a very important position, but he is in charge of the floor.

In the women's department is the senior sales clerk, Mrs. Slocombe. Her junior is Miss Brahms.

In the men's department the senior salesperson is Mr. Grainger, an old gentleman. His name, *Grainger,* is a tie-in with farmer. He is a very simple Soul, but the story today revolves around him. His assistant is Mr. Humphries, and the junior salesperson in the department is Mr. Lucas.

I'm mentioning just a few of the characters, but they work in a hierarchy. The immediate spiritual community will be the people on the sales floor and expand to include the manager, Mr. Rumbold, who has his own office, and the maintenance man who's in the union.

Each one of the different departments in the store is a small representation of a structure in society. There's

70

the union, there are the workers in the sales department, and there's the manager. But above it all is the divine power, and that's Mr. Grace, who owns the store. He comes in near the end. Together they make up the spiritual community.

Let's look at a short excerpt from the show *Coffee Morning*.

> *[Scene summary: Captain Peacock summons Mr. Grainger to his office because he took twenty minutes for his tea break instead of fifteen. Mr. Grainger says that the extra five minutes was spent in the men's room. Captain Peacock doesn't think that is a good excuse and says he will report him to the manager, Mr. Rumbold. The men's department crew rally around Mr. Grainger.]*

In this segment of the show, we've seen the complication develop. The complication is the fact that Mr. Grainger has come back to work late. The community, the rest of the men's department, form a support team. They set down a chair for him, and they get him a glass of water.

We've also seen there are several badges of authority in this community. There's the red carnation that Captain Peacock wears; there's also the tape measure around Mr. Grainger's neck. That is his badge; he is in charge of the department.

Unity Unravels

Now we're going to see if the unity of the community will stand. Or will it slowly unravel? It's not bad if something unravels, because if it comes together again it can be stronger than it was before.

In this next scene, the battle lines are drawn and the complication gets worse.

[Scene summary: Captain Peacock assembles the sales-people from both departments to read them a memo from Mr. Rumbold. To save time he has used letters of the alphabet for objects and personnel names, but it only creates more confusion. Finally the memo is read. In it Mr. Rumbold reiterates that tea breaks are to be no longer than fifteen minutes and to ensure this he is asking the personnel to sign in and out when they take breaks, even to use the bathroom. Mr. Grainger is outraged; so is the rest of the group. They decide to discuss the matter over lunch.]

Notice the communication problem when Captain Peacock reads the memo reduced to alphabet letters. Then he says, "Oh, I see (C) you (U) are (R)—" and Mrs. Slocombe says, "Are we going to start that again?" In other words, there is a complication of communication.

Keeping Our Individual Freedoms

The reason we are talking about spiritual community is that we're interested in spiritual freedom. The community is having a strong resistance to anyone taking away their freedom. Once we become Co-workers with God, we have the ultimate of freedom in whatever area we happen to find ourselves.

Mr. Grainger feels that making the staff sign in and out in a book for breaks is an outrage, and he is incensed by it. He's very angry.

In this next scene we'll see how the community bands together. But first, each one talks a little bit about what happens in their spiritual circle apart from the company. They talk about what they do at home, what their social life is like; they comment on the cafeteria food. We get to see these satellite spiritual communities which they are part of when they're not at work.

But mainly we're seeing what occurs in the lunchroom and how it affects what happens on the floor. Let's look at scene three: lunch is served.

[Scene summary: The group get their lunches and sit together. They chat for a while about the food and about their plans for the evening. Mr. Grainger interrupts to focus them on the issue of clocking in. The group sympathizes with him; how humiliating for Mr. Grainger to be dressed down in front of his coworkers. The staff argue about whether they should refuse to sign the book. But who should be first? Mr. Grainger reminds them to stick together.]

United We Stand, Divided We Fall

Mr. Grainger says something very prophetic here: "United we stand, divided we fall." They're trying to figure out how to handle this problem that is bigger than any one of them.

They're looking for leadership in this community, and they're not finding it. Should it be Mr. Grainger and Mrs. Slocombe who take the grievance to management? But even though they're senior in age and the junior staff is pushing them to do it, they don't want the responsibility.

In the next scene, we'll see the group coming out of the elevator on their way back from lunch. They push Mr. Grainger ahead of them, and he becomes the unwilling but chosen spokesman.

At this point we have the confrontation, and we'll see the community waver.

[Scene summary: Captain Peacock meets the staff as they emerge from the elevator and asks Mr. Grainger to sign the book. He refuses. Captain Peacock tells him that he shall be reported. Mr. Grainger complains

that no one else signed the book, but Captain Peacock says he only asked Mr. Grainger. Mr. Grainger is crest-fallen that no one has backed him up. He is summoned to Mr. Rumbold's office. Mr. Lucas says that they are all behind him still, but not too close.]

Mr. Lucas, the junior of the men's department, always gives the bottom line, cutting through all the social niceties and getting to what the situation really is.

Miss Brahms says, "We were going to support Mr. Grainger!" But Mrs. Slocombe starts to hedge.

The community is beginning to crumble. You'll notice every so often at work or in the family, someone offers a plan and everyone says they're all for it. But the next word is often *but*. If this is the case, you won't be getting any support there.

A Classic Case of Miscommunication

The next scene is in Mr. Rumbold's office. It is a classic case of miscommunication. Rumbold, the manager, is a character who takes everything literally. Everything goes absolutely wrong as they try to sift through the problem.

Every so often we run into someone in our spiritual community who is a Mr. Rumbold, who takes everything literally. This person cannot get the social touches down very well. Yet he or she is often in a position of authority over others, and everyone has to put up with this particular individual.

[Scene summary: Mr. Rumbold asks his secretary to take notes, so she begins to take down everything that is said, word for word. Mr. Rumbold asks Mr. Grainger if he did indeed refuse to sign the book. Mr. Grainger said, "We all refused." This doesn't matter to Mr. Rumbold, who says they must make an example of

Mr. Grainger and dock his pay by fifty pence. Mr.
Mash, the union organizer, then arrives, with a stool.]

Fifty pence is much less than fifty cents; we are dealing here in things that are really not very important. And yet they *are* very important.

Mr. Mash represents the labor union, and in this show the labor union is much better paid than everyone else. They have their own source of power, and they are strong. There's management, there's the owner of the store, and there's the labor union. The union will always figure a way to resolve the complication.

Test of Two Powers

We've seen two badges of authority so far: Captain Peacock's red carnation and Mr. Grainger's tape measure.

Now we're going to see another symbol of authority, and that is Mr. Mash's stool. He's going to organize the resistance; but he's short, and he needs to stand on something.

In the next scene there's going to be a testing of the two powers. Who's really in charge here? Is it the union as represented by Mr. Mash, or is it management as represented by Captain Peacock?

This next scene is power versus power.

[Scene summary: The staff rally around Mr. Grainger.
Some think they all ought to chip in and pay the fifty
pence. Mr. Mash, calling him Brother Grainger, says
that he has been victimized because he stood up for
his rights. Mr. Mash calls an emergency meeting of
the union members. Captain Peacock tries to pull Mr.
Grainger away, but Mr. Mash says he can't touch the
staff once they are convened. Mr. Mash lays out the
demands: remove the stigma attached to Mr. Grainger,

allow unrestricted time in the rest room, and bring the tea break system into line with current industrial practice. The vote is carried unanimously.]

Instant Karma

One of the principles of ECK is how everything comes back to you. We call it karma.

In an early scene Captain Peacock said to Mr. Grainger, "I didn't ask them to sign, I asked you." Now this is played back to him by Mr. Mash of the union.

Mr. Mash asks Captain Peacock to show his card, but Peacock says it's at home. Then Peacock wants all the union members to show their union cards during the meeting. Mash says, "You can't ask that if you don't show your card." Captain Peacock says, "You ask them to show their cards." And Mash says, "Well, now, I didn't ask them, I asked you."

It's come back to Captain Peacock.

In the next scene, Mr. Mash is going to present the community's defense to Mr. Rumbold.

You have to realize that when I speak about a community, I'm speaking about a spiritual family. These people are a spiritual family. They get together only during the workday, but people in business often spend more time with the people at work than with their own families at home.

Mr. Mash presents the argument, and Mr. Rumbold goes into the distant past to respond. Mash realizes there's no hope of reaching an agreement, so he says something vulgar. When logic fails, the union resorts to force.

[Scene summary: Rumbold tells Mr. Mash that there is no possibility of Grace Brothers acceding to the group's demands, that there's no reason to even discuss it.]

The Community Pulls Together

In the next scene Mash is going to orchestrate the resistance even more. But as he does, the community will begin to rise up against his plan. You'll see the community start to gather up the threads of its unity again.

But before things get better, they get worse. Mr. Grainger is more than ever the outcast, both from his fellow workers and from Captain Peacock, his immediate supervisor. The community is about as broken as it can be, but there are also some signs that it's going to come back together again.

[Scene summary: Mr. Mash gathers the staff, saying that they have to resist together by slowing down their work. But Mrs. Slocombe wants to get her work done so she can catch her bus. Mash tells her to leave everything as is, but she says she doesn't want to lose her customers and her commission. "We all have to make sacrifices," says Mash, but she refuses. At the close of the scene, the staff is grumbling about the union decision.]

Individual Dignity

Poor Mr. Grainger is the sweetest man, even though he's grumpy. He expresses himself in his own way.

There is a strong disagreement in this community, but they still allow each other their dignity. Even when Mr. Mash uses his vulgarisms, he does it within limits so he can still retain his sense of dignity.

A spiritual community is strong when the individual members allow the other members to retain their dignity. And the community breaks down in the face of disagreement when people begin to make fun or break down the dignity of different members of the family.

77

The dignity of the individual is very important on a path such as ECKANKAR. We have our own disagreements; but there is a right way to go about getting resolution, and there are hundreds of wrong ways to do it.

A Heartless Plan

In the last scene Mrs. Slocombe is the first one to say she doesn't like this plan as much as she did in the beginning. She's got to save up for the holidays, and if this union plan means she's not going to work, then forget it. All of a sudden you see that the union plan is a good plan but a heartless one.

The next scene is at lunch again, and we're going to see the lull before the storm hits.

[Scene summary: Mr. Mash sits with the group at lunch. The staff talks about how they tried to go slow that morning, but it hasn't been a success. Mash says, "In that case we'll have to escalate." He suggests hijacking the elevator with Rumbold inside it. Mr. Grainger objects, as does Mrs. Slocombe. They begin blaming each other.]

Perfect Justice

Grainger is the leader after all. He doesn't want to be, but he is.

In this last scene, justice is done. We're going to see another part of the spiritual community, young Mr. Grace. Young Mr. Grace is justice. He's the owner of the company, and he shows up and sets things right. He resolves the problem.

He does it differently than the union or management — he doesn't use compromise. He makes a resolution that goes one step beyond what anybody else expected. And he is very agreeable with everyone, even with Mr. Mash who's trying to be disagreeable.

When it all ends, you'll find that justice is perfect justice, but it's not what anyone expected. The problem is resolved. The community is reunited, but it's a little different at the end than it was at the beginning.

> *[Scene summary: Mr. Rumbold and Captain Peacock are approached by Mr. Mash, and he gives an ultimatum: unless the demands are accepted, everyone leaves. Then Young Mr. Grace arrives; he'd just gotten a copy of Rumbold's memo about the tea breaks. Mash presents his argument, and Rumbold presents his. But Mr. Grace surprisingly agrees with Mash that tea breaks should begin when the staff sits down to eat. Everyone believes they have won, and they say that they were behind Mr. Grainger the whole way. Then Mr. Grace goes on to say that they will have their tea brought to them at their work stations. Basically, they have lost their tea break completely.]*

Seeing Yourself

I hope by looking at this you were able to see yourself better, and your family, the people you work with, the people you spend recreational time with. As the credits run, we see the faces of the different individuals. Because the spiritual family is ultimately made up of individuals, each one having dignity and worth.

Worship is living every day in a community of others.

This is true worship; it's not just the Sabbath break we take from our lives to go to church or temple. It's living every day in a community with others. And it's every community.

79

Our Spiritual Destiny

In the family, we're working out problems to become better people. We're becoming more purified individuals so that one day we can take a place above even the rank of angels and go on to help serve God and our fellow creatures.

A Co-worker with God is a servant of life.

This is why *Are You Being Served?* was an appropriate title for this demonstration of what a spiritual community is. A spiritual community can be made up of Lutherans, Catholics, ECKists, even atheists or agnostics. Because a spiritual community includes all people on earth in different circles of different sizes.

Each time you move from the circle of the home to the circle of school or business, you are entering a whole new world. There you will run into people who are working out their problems. While they are working out their problems, you are also working out your own.

This is how the Law of Karma works in everyday living. The end result is that we are to become people of love and compassion who allow other people to be themselves.

I hope this helps you recognize yourself as part of a number of different spiritual communities as you go about your life. Once you can recognize the spiritual community you are part of, then you will recognize that you are worshiping whenever you treat other people with respect, as divine beings, as Soul.

*ECK Worship Service, Temple of ECK,
Chanhassen, Minnesota, Sunday, January 5, 1992*

The woman walked to a hilltop where she had often gone since her husband died and stood there watching the lights. Soon she began to hear the very quiet sound of tinkling bells.

7

Night of the Bells

It's been somewhat of a rough year for most; the recession has left its mark on a number of you, more than would like to be included in that number. But even though it has been hard on some people, maybe it's also necessary.

Seeing More Clearly

We get to look things over and see what we don't really need in our lives. It's a good time for self-evaluation of a spiritual kind. You can get rid of those things that are not necessary, just get them out of your life. If they haven't helped you in the past, they probably won't help you in the future.

During times of hardship, we have this exceptional ability to see things more clearly than we do in prosperous times.

So, as much as possible, look at this as an opportunity. Sometimes that's all you can do. When things look bad, you say, "Maybe I'm just not seeing the silver lining." Look for it, and you'll find it.

Visiting Friends

We had snow so early in Minneapolis this winter that even the sparrows left. A big snowfall came right after the ECK Worldwide Seminar, and another came in November after the ECK South Pacific Seminar. I guess the sparrows went south, but now they're back, with their children.

It's getting vicious at our backyard bird feeder. We have a young cardinal who wants to take over territory from his dad. The dad cardinal homesteaded there. He's a beautiful bird; he'll sit by his territory and fluff out his chest to let everyone—especially his children—know that this is his area, that they should go find another feeding dish. But they don't want to because our dish is always full.

Surprise Tactics

We've also had a pheasant with us through the winter. The pheasant is a large game bird that looks very silly when it runs. It looks like a cartoon: it puts its head up, goes "Ock!" then shoots away.

The pheasant is also a stealthy bird. I'll watch our pheasant coming through his little patch of wood, very quietly and carefully. Usually the red and gray squirrels, the rabbits, and the other wildlife are at the feeding dish, but they don't notice the pheasant because of his beautiful camouflage feathers. Then he gives this terrible honk. The rabbits jump straight up in the air, and the squirrels dash off. Pretty soon the area is cleared, and the pheasant can walk up and eat.

My wife and I enjoy watching our family—the birds and other creatures. But I hide a lot from them now. I put the feed out when they're not there. All they know is that the dish is always full. They don't know who their God is, who provides the food.

Their Hideous God

Once in a while I make a mistake. I forget what time it is, maybe because I've been working on something. I'll think it's time to feed the birds and animals, so I go to the back door where the feed is stored. One time I opened up the door and startled a winter rabbit and a gray squirrel. They acted as if they had seen the great monster from the other side. When I came back in, I told my wife, "I think I am their hideous God."

Paul Twitchell wrote about the hideous God in *The Tiger's Fang*. Some of you may have read this book about the spiritual journey that Paul Twitchell made to God Consciousness.

Often people are like these birds and animals out in the backyard. They pray to God, they praise God, and they thank God for the food and bountiful blessings. But if God were ever to show his face, or her face, or its face—whatever they believe God to be—they would practically fall over from sheer fright. Because they never imagined their God could be so hideous.

The birds and animals get their food from their hideous God who stands behind this curtain. They never see him. They couldn't stand the shock; they couldn't separate the gift from the giver, except to say, "The gift is good, and the giver is hideous."

To a pheasant, I suppose God looks like another pheasant, except bigger. And I don't fit the pheasant family. The pheasant probably prays to his pheasant God, the great blessed winged father of all pheasants. Then one day he sees me putting out the food, and he can't believe his eyes. He runs off ten steps, then stops and turns back to look one more time. "Yup. Ugly as I thought," he probably says, then runs off.

God's True Glory

People are like that, too, from what I've observed. They all have their notions about God.

They put together some human characteristics they admire, some noble traits and qualities—and there aren't very many. If the human mind can come up with it, you know there's a lot missing. But they put the best they can forward and say this is God, the great God of all goodness.

I wonder if God ever showed ITSELF to people, how many could stand the sight of God, in God's true glory. Most of them, of course, feel they could take it very easily. I imagine when the pheasant prays, he says the same thing to his family.

A Lesson from Nature

One day I ran out of birdseed. "I don't know what to do until tomorrow when the store's open," I told my wife. "If you want to give them some of my shredded wheat, you can," she said.

Shredded wheat was her special cereal. She'd been eating it a lot, with fruit and other things on it. She just loved it.

So I filled two bowls with shredded wheat and carried them outside to the feeding area. A couple of hours later we looked out the window; the dishes were still full. There were plenty of tracks in the snow leading up to the shredded wheat, but nobody had touched it.

The next morning it was still there, and there were a lot more tracks. So I went to the store and bought some birdseed. We threw away the shredded wheat. After that I noticed my wife didn't eat her special cereal as often. She figured that if the birds and animals won't touch it, maybe there isn't much value in it. Some very wise beings in the neighborhood tested it and didn't give it their stamp of approval.

You learn from nature. Sometimes the lessons you learn are very good ones, but they can catch you totally off guard.

Animals and People

Animals, birds, and people are pretty much alike, because we're all Soul.

People often take this as a sacrilegious statement. They believe humankind is God's highest creation. But anyone who has studied human beings or their behavior would be rolling on the floor at that thought. They'd say you had a good sense of humor.

The first anthropological studies of apes seemed to indicate that the papa gorilla was very kind and fair to his family, that he took care of the mama and the babies. But they've recently found that gorilla families have just as many different characteristics as humans do. Some gorillas are kind and show a great deal of compassion; others are just plain brutes.

This is pretty much the same as we find among human beings: some are compassionate and some are brutes.

It's a dog-eat-dog world for all Souls—birds, animals, and humans. We try to get along in life. We try to mark out a little spot for ourselves, a favorite place at home, our chair that has all the cookie crumbs and tea or coffee spills. We tell everyone else not to touch it. The family members stay away, but the cats and dogs will jump up there.

Just Show Love

Cats like to be where we are because they figure if it's good enough for a human, it's good enough for a cat. Of all living creatures, cats feel they have the most right to anything, even more than you do.

Dogs have a different reason. They just like to be near the place where their beloved master sat. Dogs simply love you for what you are.

I like cats; I like dogs too. But they are different, and you have to understand that. People who love cats and people who love dogs can learn a lot about themselves by seeing who they love.

But when it comes to love, don't think too much about it. If you just love someone or something, that's more than many people are able to do.

Sugarbear

My daughter's friend has a little dog named Sugarbear. Everyone picked on this dog—cats, dogs, even kittens.

Sugarbear recently began to have some strange behavior. For some reason she would run out into the middle of the road, spray a little, then sit there. Cars would stop, honk, and slowly drive around. She sat there until she felt like coming back into the yard.

My daughter and her friend would try to get Sugarbear to come out of the road. They wondered, *Is Sugarbear losing her mind?* Maybe the world had beaten up on her so much that she was losing her reason.

One day my daughter saw a cat walk up to the house, spray a bush to mark his territory, then walk away. Pretty soon a dog came walking up, sniffed at the bush, and sprayed it too. He had recaptured the territory for his own. Finally a little kitten came along after the dog and marked the bush for herself.

About this time, Sugarbear came out of the house. She sniffed the bush and realized that it had already been claimed by some greater power. So she ran into the middle of the road and marked her territory out there. Nobody else wanted that territory, so she didn't have a lot of competition.

People sometimes wonder why the explorers got in their little boats and went sailing off into the unknown. There were significant dangers involved and not many creature comforts. But they were like little Sugarbear going out in the middle of the road. They needed freedom, and they couldn't find it in the towns and settlements. So they went where no one else had the courage to go.

Driving Force of Freedom

When the mountain men went into the American West and established new settlements, the merchants and townspeople would eventually follow. They admired these early explorers and wondered why they would make these journeys into unknown territories. Many of the explorers never made it back. Others spent their whole lives going to the farthest extreme they could.

Basically the driving force for this is freedom. They wanted freedom, and the risks were not enough to hold them back.

Sometimes people ask, "What does the Mahanta, the Living ECK Master do in his spare time?" I say, "First of all, I try to help people find their way home to God." But the other part I enjoy so much is exploring the Far Country.

The Outer Master is the person you see right here, sitting in this comfortable chair. The Inner Master is the counterpart of this, working on the inner planes to help those who want to learn more about themselves. People who have the courage to go into their own dreamland, to poke around in the corners and find out what's there. To get in boats, take rides on great rivers—to ride the great river to the ocean and someday see the face of God.

Life Is Choice

In 1965 when ECKANKAR came out, contemplation was a word very few people understood. It was associated with weird Eastern religions. Today it's part of the mainstream. People are having near-death and other experiences, and contemplation is a commonplace thing now.

One of the Higher Initiates went into contemplation by chanting her secret word, or you can use HU. She asked the Inner Master, "How do you find time to deal with all the needs and cares of all beings?" Instead of giving her a direct answer, he gave her a picture.

The Higher Initiate was taken out of the body in Soul Travel and looked down on a scene. She saw a school bus coming down a country road. The bus stopped, and a child got out and began to run home through a forest area. And the Higher Initiate saw a wolf stalking the girl.

The woman said to the Inner Master, "Can you protect the child from the wolf?" So the Master let a rabbit run in front of the wolf. The wolf went after the rabbit, and the child was safe.

The Higher Initiate felt uneasy about this. "Did it have to be a bunny?" she asked.

The Master said to her, "Life is choice. Life is one choice, and another choice, and another choice. What is the difference if I provide a rabbit for the dinner of the girl's family or a rabbit to the wolf? Everything has needs, and there's always a choice." In this case, the choice was the freedom and welfare of the child.

Love or Power?

This awesome power of life and death is the same power that every Soul has. It's the power to use or abuse, always there in some degree. We hope that if someone is not very unfolded spiritually, that person doesn't get too much power. Power without love creates people like Hitler.

The pure balance of the Holy Spirit is power and love, but mostly love. God is love. This is what we are trying to develop within ourselves.

Whenever I see people moving toward the polarity of power, I can foresee all the problems they're going to cause, first for others, then for themselves.

But if I see someone going on the path of love, I see a bright future for that individual. That person will be doing a lot of good for other people. And this good will come back in the way of spiritual unfoldment and enlightenment.

It's amazing how many people in a spiritual teaching—including ECKANKAR—go for the path of power at some time or another. It's their lesson, they need to do it as part of their spiritual training. They have to learn that there is something higher, better, and more powerful than power. The more powerful thing is pure love.

The Wrong Kind of Love

We've all had our share of the wrong kind of love. Under this category I would put the so-called missionaries who go into a society to change the people and their morals. Why do they do that?

One of the most absurd examples were the European missionaries who went to Hawaii, a very hot climate, and put clothes on all the people because the missionaries were ashamed of themselves. To them, it was a noble deed. They also practiced some of the most brutal methods imaginable if the people didn't accept their message of salvation.

I practically cry when I see the brutality of people who are acting in the name of God. Theirs must indeed be a hideous God.

If they had the eyes to see what they were doing to another human being, they would see it's an awful thing. But they are proud of it; they put it into their history books. To me it is one of the saddest statements of a religion that teaches love, but practices the abuse of power.

Growing Closer to God

In our past lives as Christians, Buddhists, Muslims, Jains, or students of the primitive animist religions, if we haven't learned how to allow other people freedom of being, then we haven't learned very much about God. There is still a wall of separation between that Soul and God.

So then, what is God?

God is the unknowable. I could give thirty-five adjectives that explain what God is not or what God is. But it still wouldn't be God. God is pretty much what you imagine God to be, right now. When you grow and unfold over the years, God will still be pretty much what you think God is. Maybe a whole lot more. And maybe even a whole lot less.

Night of the Bells

A short article ran in *Reader's Digest* called "Night of the Bells." A woman on a ranch in South Dakota had lost her husband a short time before. One night in March she had a dream and woke up about 1:00 a.m. She didn't realize what time it was when she woke, and she wondered if it was dawn yet. Without her husband, the nights were long and she missed him.

So she got up, went out on the deck, and looked to the north. In the sky she saw waves of blue and white light, the northern lights.

The deck had frost on it, so she went back indoors to get the sheepskin moccasins her husband had made for her. When she came back out, the northern lights were less strong. She wondered if they were going away.

But then they came in stronger colors, reds, greens, blues. They were so beautiful. The woman stood there watching them, realizing that this was a sacred moment. So she walked to a hilltop where she had often gone since her husband died and stood there watching the lights.

Soon she began to hear the very quiet sound of tinkling bells.

The sound of bells became stronger whenever the woman saw flashes of green light. She thought they sounded like glass wind chimes, but there was no wind that night.

Then she remembered stories from arctic travelers who had seen the northern lights and heard a sound at the same time. And the woman wondered what the sound was. But aside from the arctic explorers and herself, she had never heard anyone make a reference to the sound. And she ended the article by saying some things were meant to be mysterious.

The woman didn't understand that this was the Voice of God.

The Voice of God comes to people in one form as the Sound and Light. And the Sound can be the tinkling of bells at a certain level on the inner planes. It usually happens on the Causal Plane when you are remembering the past.

What was the woman doing when she heard the bells? She was missing her husband, she was remembering the past. Where was she? On the Causal Plane, where the seed of all cause and effect that occurs in a person's life is stored.

Importance of Sound

In contemplation, when you chant HU or your secret word, I encourage you to look and listen for the Voice of God, which we call the ECK.

This is what Christianity calls the Holy Spirit. But Christianity has reduced the Holy Spirit to a person, the Holy Ghost. The Holy Spirit is not a person; it's the action of divine Light and Sound, God speaking to creation.

Creation exists because of the waves of vibration. And this vibration at different levels is Light and Sound. Without this divine vibration coming from the Ocean of Love and Mercy, or God, there would be no life.

People can get along without light but they cannot get along without sound.

You can put people in a dark room without light, and it's frightening but they get along. But it's very hard for people to exist without sound.

Survival is perhaps the highest driving force within the human being. When prisoners of war were put into solitary confinement, the ones who survived were able to visualize something—some practiced a hobby or saw stories like movies in their inner vision.

They were looking through the eyes of Soul.

They were looking at something real, as real as their prison cell but at a different level. And thus they were able to survive.

Practicing HU

HU is one of the most sacred names for God. If you sing it, it'll give you the spiritual insight that other people wish they had. But it doesn't come overnight. You have to develop it like any other skill.

If you ever get yourself in a place where you need hope, where you're cut off from communication with loved ones, sing HU with love and reverence.

Look for the Light and listen for the Sound of God. It may come as the tinkling of bells.

ECK Springtime Seminar, Washington, D.C.,
Friday, April 17, 1992

When things are not going well, you might sing HU. It's a love song to God, a connection between Soul and the Divine Being.

8

HU for All You Do

At ECK seminars, we try to speak about why this life is worth living, what help you can get from God and the Holy Spirit to help you through it, and how to go about getting this help.

Life's Little Problems

One of the things I have to put up with is putting on powder before I come out here. This is so the video cameras don't pick up shiny spots on my head where the hair has gotten thinner through worry and other impacts of life. My wife very carefully applies the powder, and I tell her, "Lightly, lightly," because years ago when they were first powdering me before talks, they put it on pretty heavily. I could literally crack a smile.

As she was powdering my face, I was thinking about tonight's talk. It was going through my mind very quickly. She wanted to make sure she didn't get powder in my eyes, so she asked me to shut them. "Shut!" she said again. I thought they were shut, but I was thinking about things. So I opened them to see what was going on.

"Shut!" my wife said. "I had them shut before," I said.

97

"I saw your eyelids moving," she said. "People do that when they dream," I told her.

We deal with life, and usually our problems are little things like this rather than big and heavy things. You can work with them, thankful that the big problems are somewhere else right now.

Daisy and the Feed Dish

We have two ducks that come to our backyard feeder. They were the first two that arrived, so we named them Donald and Daisy, of course. Daisy upsets me because she's eating so much; she's trying to bulk up so she can lay all her eggs. Next year we'll have to figure out how to feed all those offspring too.

I set the food out at night, and the raccoons come. They have tiny little hands, and they sift through the seed, so they don't eat a whole lot. Then the rabbits come. Finally, at first light, the gray squirrels and the red squirrels are out there. Everyone eats all night long and during the day. And there's still food in the dishes. But then Donald and Daisy arrive.

Daisy can clean out both dishes in ten minutes, then look at the window where I work. Sometimes she looks at me as if she'd like to come inside and clean out our kitchen too.

One cold day I felt sorry for her. The ground had been bare of snow for several days but we had had a snowfall that night. "No food for the ducks with this snow," I told my wife. "I think I'd better go out and give Daisy some more seed."

When Daisy saw me she did a very interesting thing: She waddled off a few feet from me, then lay flat down and put her neck straight out on the lawn. I imagine that's what she does to hide when the lawn is brown, since she's a brown duck. But she looked kind of ridiculous on top of the snow.

"Daisy," I told her, "you're not fooling anybody." Have you ever seen a duck look sheepish?

Spiritual Food

Part of my job is to put food out for the animals and the birds. At the same time, I'm also here to put spiritual food out for people. It's pretty much the same thing.

Some people look as if they might eat a lot, but they don't. Then a whole lot of others do a good job of eating. And some like Daisy need more feed. Sometimes it strains my ability and my wallet trying to keep up with an appetite like that.

But I find there is always a way.

I thought buying a fifty-pound bag of feed was a lot. Then my sister wrote; she feeds flocks of geese. It started out with a few and turned into flocks. I know what ducks can eat; I can't imagine what flocks of geese would consume.

ECK on Computer

Some of the ECKists are working on-line with computers now. They meet for an on-line class once a month. You enter a discussion area on the computer, room E-C-K, and as you come into the room, the computer tells you who else is there. Someone greets you, and then you talk about ECK.

It's for people who want to know about ECK and get together with each other.

Talking on computers is a funny thing because you have to learn to condense your thoughts. You get four or five people together, and everyone types a line and asks questions. You're reading a message from somebody who wrote it two minutes before. It's a stream of consciousness; you have to pick out who said what, and it's a strange experience.

Winning the Raffle

I got a letter from a friend in California who's a Higher Initiate. He always put himself at the cutting edge of life. He would try new things.

When he was younger and he did things for ECK, he didn't always know if something was exactly in accord with the way the Holy Spirit really works or not. But it didn't stop him from trying things.

For a while people would mop up after him. He gradually learned what ECK was all about and how the Holy Spirit worked so he could express himself properly. For the past five or ten years, he's done very well. He's still telling people about the Light and Sound, and how singing HU can help them.

The local symphony orchestra was having a raffle to raise money, and tickets were one hundred dollars each. The first prize was a new BMW. "I could use a nice car," the ECKist said, so he bought a ticket.

Then he bent the principles of ECK a little bit.

We don't use HU or visualization techniques in ECK to gain something for ourselves materially. We sing HU to open ourselves as a channel for the Holy Spirit. But the ECKist was making an experiment, and he did it very nicely.

He began to visualize the car, saying, "I'm going to make that BMW part of my world." He got a dummy key and held it all the time. He even went to a BMW dealer once a month for a test drive. "I can't help but win that car if I put my whole attention on it," he said. So he did.

He put 100 percent of himself into this dream.

And this is how we do life in ECK. We try to do it 100 percent. A precious lifetime.

It's an experiment and an experience in time and space. We make the best of it if we can.

The symphony orchestra planned to sell six hundred of these tickets, but they were able to sell only about four hundred and fifty. And then comes the news.

He didn't win the BMW. He won second prize: two plane tickets to Paris.

And coincidentally, for the first time we were having the ECK European Seminar in Paris that summer. The ECK, the Holy Spirit, works these things out, not as we will but as It will.

So the ECKist went. He said he was very happy to have won the plane tickets.

What's Best for You Spiritually

Whatever you want in life is going to take some effort on your part.

The greater your dream, the more you're going to have to work to get it. In some way, you'll have to put forth effort.

Put forth the effort, but then be willing to be surprised at what kind of return you get. Because if you open your heart completely to the divine influence in your life, you'll find the blessings come to you.

The Holy Spirit decides what's best for you, what you need for your spiritual unfoldment. Apparently, this ECKist needed two tickets to Paris.

Future Visions

Euro Disneyland just opened east of Paris. Some of the Europeans like it, some don't.

If you ever go to Disneyland, you'll find it's very much like the Astral Plane. It's a beautiful place. The animals talk just like in the cartoons. The artists go to the Astral Plane to come up with these creations. There's a huge museum of invention there, with a prototype of any invention that's ever been or will be.

I like museums, although there is an awful heaviness in some of them. But I think the museum of natural history would be a fantastic place to visit. Scientists are studying where human beings came from. They do studies with primates and see if there is a link between human beings and apes.

What they're doing is trying to get the fine shadings of things that walk on two legs. Eventually they'll stumble on the real question: Where did the first ones come from anyway?

I don't like to talk about it too much, yet ours is a teaching where you can look into many different things. And I think it won't be too many years before we're going to find out that we're not alone in this universe, that people have been traveling back and forth. All the Trekkies, the people who like *Star Trek,* are going to be the visionaries; everyone else will play catch-up.

A Fisherman's Story

One of the African initiates wrote me about how singing HU had helped him in his personal life. HU, the sacred name for God, is a special word. Money was short, and there wasn't enough to buy food for the family the next day. But his hobby was fishing, so the man decided he would go fishing to get food.

He got on a bus late at night that went out to a lagoon. When he got there, he put on all his fishing gear and walked out into the lagoon. After he had caught enough fish to feed his family, he sat for a while on the beach, resting before getting the bus back home.

Suddenly he saw a tall man coming down the beach.

In the moonlight, the ECKist saw something shiny glinting at the man's side. The man came up to him and said, "My friend, what are you doing here at night?"

Close up, the initiate could see a long knife in a scabbard on the man's hip, so the ECKist began chanting HU quietly to himself and didn't answer the man. The stranger thought, *This fisherman must not speak English*, so he tried one of the native languages. Still the ECKist did not respond. So the tall man switched back to English.

Finally the ECKist said, "I am here fishing with my friends."

"That's strange," said the tall man. "Before I came up to you, I looked all over and didn't see anyone else. Where are your friends?"

"Over there," said the ECKist, pointing off in the dark down the beach.

"I don't see anyone," said the tall man.

"Well, look again," said the ECKist, and he kept chanting HU.

Suddenly the tall man started counting out loud, "One, two." When the ECKist looked down the beach, he couldn't see anything at first, but then he began to see people coming down the beach toward them. The man kept counting, "Three, four." And the ECKist saw more people walking toward them.

Soon there was a whole crowd of people coming along the beach. The tall man quickly looked around, backed away from the ECKist, and took to his heels into the night.

The ECKist looked over at the people coming down the beach, and they melted away into nothingness. They just disappeared. Then he realized what he had so often heard from the Mahanta was true: "You are not alone. I am always with you."

What the Saints Had

It's a case of protection. I get many letters like this from people who have found help from one of the ECK Masters or have been helped spiritually through an illness. Sometimes the help comes in the dream state, sometimes directly via Soul Travel.

Soul Travel offers a wide range of experiences. Sometimes it can be as simple as having an impression or intuitive feeling about something. Sometimes it can be stronger, like being above the physical body.

People who do the Spiritual Exercises of ECK often find themselves above the body, much as the saints used to in the early Christian teachings.

There are accounts of levitation among early Christian saints, but most Christians aren't aware of this. When certain things do not fit into church history, the church fathers or scribes very carefully delete this or that passage. But every few decades or so, a new person comes along who has these manifestations of miracles.

ECK is not about miracles, basically. It's about finding God.

In the Christian Bible it says, Seek ye first the kingdom of heaven and all things shall be added unto you. This is what we are looking for—to reach the kingdom of heaven in this lifetime. The way to do this is through the Spiritual Exercises of ECK.

The mainstay of these exercises is the word HU, an ancient name for God. Once secret, still sacred. It works.

When to Chant HU

You don't have to be an ECKist to chant HU. And you don't have to chant HU. Just simply try to find God at some very pleasant time. Bedtime is good because everything has settled down. Your outer life is quiet.

Other times to chant HU are when you are in trouble, as with the ECKist fisherman. When things are not going well at the office, when you've had a bad day or someone else is having a bad day and you happen to be lower on the pecking order, you might sing HU.

It's a love song to God, a connection between Soul and the Divine Being, the Ancient of Days. If you really care about finding truth, sing HU.

Beyond Dogma

So many people who have only the dogma of their religion feel that truth is in the dogma. They become very upset when people have dreams or other interpretations of truth which conflicts with that dogma.

Most dogma was created long ago. It has often been left in the dust of time. But people change, and new conditions come along.

The Holy Spirit works with people every moment. To find God, you don't need to rely only on scriptures that are several thousand years old. In fact, since so few people are finding God along the old routes, maybe it's time to try something new.

Take a Test Drive

But you don't bet the farm on a dream.

You don't just throw your present religion away and say, "I'm going to join ECKANKAR or some other path." You don't just throw the past away. It's easier on yourself—and even more educational and in tune with nature—to try to make a smooth transition.

Try something new out; take it for a test drive. See if it works. Test it every step of the way.

If it works for you, you're going to gain more confidence in yourself as a spiritual being. You're going to find you *are* a spiritual being, that you are Soul. Not that you have a Soul. That belief is dead old dogma that is doing no one any good.

People do not have Soul; people are Soul, and they have bodies.

If you can make this jump in understanding through singing HU or some other way, you will have gained more in a lifetime than many of the people who set themselves up as leaders of orthodox religions. Many of them don't know about the Light and Sound of God.

How We Hear God's Voice

A few instances in the Bible mention the Light and Sound. But those few instances are like the tip of the iceberg. It's only the beginning.

Hearing the sound of tinkling bells in conjunction with the northern lights is one example. Other people hear the sound of a flute. All these are sounds of God.

The Sound of God comes to people through the Holy Spirit, which is the Voice of God. And one of the highest ways God speaks to people is through the Sound and Light.

Not through angels or any other way, but through the Sound and Light to lead people home to God.

True Value, True Love

Sometimes ECKists become complacent. They get lazy. They know that singing HU can help them in their daily life. But it's like anything else, like a good spouse. You can take the good spouse for granted. And you forget that what builds a relationship is love.

How does love work?

It's sometimes holding your tongue when you'd rather not. It means being a little more patient, a little more understanding. It means giving your spouse the benefit of the doubt even as your spouse does the same for you when you're not feeling well.

Any expression of love, of true love, expresses divine love. That is why the path of ECK is the path of love. It's live and let live.

An Exercise for Depression

Someone wrote to me about depression. It is a common thing. A lot of people don't realize that it comes most often during the winter months because we don't get enough light. We need light, the right kind of light.

This person would do the spiritual exercises while lying in bed at night. She would put her attention on the Spiritual Eye. This is at the forehead, roughly between and slightly above the eyebrows. Then she would quiet herself down and begin to chant HU.

She would start singing out loud, then after three or four minutes she'd feel like singing silently. So she would.

After another five minutes or so, she'd suddenly feel

that she wanted to just be still. The saying in the Bible is, "Be still, and know that I am God." So she'd just be still, and wait and watch.

If you want to try this, you can imagine yourself sitting by a river, listening to it flow gently by. Or you can just sit there. Quietly watch and wait. After a while, you'll feel it's time to open your eyes.

If nothing happens the first time, try again. You may try this exercise thirty times in a month before you have any success. Or it may take you two or three months. You may not want to do it every night. You might want to try it every other night. But try it. Remember, there is power and love in the word *HU*.

HU is another way of saying, "May the blessings be."

ECK Springtime Seminar, Washington, D.C.,
Saturday, April 18, 1992

Because she had asked the Mahanta, "Help me serve;
help me love," the riches of ECK had come to her.

9

The Riches of ECK

I was talking last night with someone who grew up Catholic. He used to have a lot of discussions with the priests about what happened when people die. He would say, "I'm going to heaven," and the priests would say, "No, when you die your Soul goes to heaven."

But the man wouldn't buy it. He knew he was more than just a physical body who had a Soul.

Basic Beliefs

Even as a young child, he recognized that he was Soul. So when he heard about ECKANKAR, it made sense. One of our basic tenets and beliefs is that each person is Soul. We take on this body, and at death we drop it to go on to the higher planes. But the priests said something different, and this made for some very hard feelings.

Sometimes the people who are put in positions of spiritual leadership in religions don't really understand the spiritual way of life.

Snow Throwers

It's spring here in North America. At least in some areas the snow is just about gone. The last place the glaciers must have melted was on our lawn. For the second year in a row, we have snow longer than anyone else in the neighborhood.

Our neighbor across the street has a huge snow thrower. It is a monstrous thing. These past two years when we've had a good amount of snow, he hasn't had hardly any. He cleans his driveway in no time flat, then looks at ours with envy.

I have a medium-sized snow thrower. I bought it because snow in Minnesota can last six months. The very first snowstorm this year, my snow thrower lost its teeth, and it wouldn't throw snow. "Poor thing," I said. "A couple of years of mild winters, and now it's forgotten how to eat snow."

Taking Care of Things

One morning while my wife was still in bed, I lugged the broken snow thrower into the kitchen. From years of living on a farm, I do not like to work on machines outside in the cold. While the snow thrower thawed, I began reading the book of instructions on how to repair it. They were difficult to understand. "I hope the ECK teachings are clearer than this," I said.

I torture myself whenever there is work to be done on the computer or the snow thrower. I pull out the book of instructions and study it, believing it will help. My wife knows better; she just calls somebody and says, "This doesn't work. Could you fix it, please?"

The fact is, when my wife calls someone for service help, I'm embarrassed to listen. "No human being could know so little about a machine," I say.

But it works. She has never had a problem with repair people. "It's not the same for a man as it is for a woman," I tell her. I may get letters saying I'm sexist, but some people have gone blind in the last twenty years; they don't realize there is a difference.

So I took the instruction manual upstairs and read it for as long as I could. I thought that if I can make the ECK teachings and the spiritual exercises simpler than that instruction manual, I'd do it.

I figured two people had put that manual together: an illustrator and a copywriter. And neither of them had ever seen the machine.

I put the manual aside, picked up my wrench, and opened up the snow thrower. The machine broke in half and flipped parts on the floor. Then I looked inside and saw all these V-belts. "Hey, I know V-belts," I said. "They've got to be tight." So I tightened everything and put the snow thrower back together again.

And it worked.

More Freedom

To me, the riches of ECK is being able to fix my snow thrower. To me this is a gift. The more you can do for yourself, the more freedom you have.

It's very easy to call someone on the phone and say, "Come over and fix this, please." Sometimes you have to do that because you don't have time away from your job to fix things and spend time with your family. And you want to spend time with your family, so you have somebody else fix things.

But it's good to learn about the essential things, things that would be a real inconvenience if they broke down. We pick our projects. The spiritual principle behind this is spiritual freedom. We want to be independent and not rely on others for things we can do ourselves.

Yet at the same time, we realize that this is what gives

113

us our strength. So that when we see someone else who needs help, we can give it when they need it. And when we aren't strong, others can help us. This helping back and forth is what builds the community of ECK.

The Perfect Job

A woman wrote me recently. For years she'd been in one poorly paying job after another. It was simply because she'd gotten into the job market too late in her life; she didn't have as good a work history as she might have had if she had started working very young.

One night she asked the Inner Master, "Could you get me a job where I can help other people that would also be fulfilling to me? Where I could give love to people and love doing what I do?"

The very next morning when she was reading through the want ads, a little blue light appeared next to one particular ad.

Sometimes this little Blue Star of ECK appears for people. It's the light pen of the Mahanta, saying, "Here, look at this item." It puts attention on that thing or whatever you're doing. It says, "This is best for your spiritual interests right now."

The job seemed too good: work half a year for a full year's wages. She knew that if something sounded too good to be true, it probably was. So she read on.

Mahanta's Light Pen

But the little blue light stayed next to that ad, and eventually the woman gave in. She called the number that was listed in the ad and found the job was being a houseparent for several retarded adults. When she went to interview for the job, she met the young people and saw the twinkle of Soul in their eyes. Later she told me, "Never in my imagination could I have found a job opportunity that suits me as well as this one."

Because she had asked the Mahanta, "Help me serve; help me love," the riches of ECK had come to her.

Three Trucks

The riches of ECK also come in the dream state. An initiate found herself with the Inner Master one night and the Master was showing her a newspaper photo of a truck. As she was looking at the newspaper, something jogged her memory. Three times in the past month she had seen a big truck driving down the road; each time the truck would suddenly go off the road, do a sharp U-turn, and get back on the road again. The drivers hadn't even seemed to pay much attention to the near accidents.

When she woke up, she thought about the dream and the three trucks. She asked the Inner Master, "What do these three trucks mean?"

"I think that's something you have to find out for yourself," he answered.

This answer took her by surprise. So she began looking at her daily life and found she wasn't very careful about details. She drifted here and there, and the next thing she knew, she was off track. If she would plan more carefully, she realized, she wouldn't get off on all these sidetracks. She would stay on the road.

This woman is a very easygoing person who gets along well with others and is able to work with them. She was worried that she was not keeping on track, but she was actually doing very well up to that point. It was just that now she had given up those responsibilities of a certain kind of leadership, and the Mahanta was saying, "It would be a little easier on you now if you made a plan and went for it, if you drove straight ahead and didn't wander off the road."

Often the Inner Master comes and gives you instructions three times, often in three different ways. Especially if it's an important spiritual insight for you, you'll get it three times. But you have to be aware enough to notice when the insight or dream comes.

This is why I so often recommend that initiates in ECK keep a dream journal or a journal of their lives.

The Riches of ECK

Another ECKist had a dream where she was walking her dog down a street. In the dream she came upon a very old, large suitcase. Since nobody seemed to own it, the woman decided to take it home. As she began to carry it down the street, a man walked up to her. "May I help?" he asked.

The ECKist recognized him as Paul Twitchell, the ECK Master who brought out ECKANKAR in 1965 and translated, or died, in 1971.

"Thank you very much," she said, handing him the heavy suitcase.

"I'll help you carry it home," said Paul, but when they got very close to her house, he set the suitcase on the ground. "You'll have to carry it the rest of the way yourself," he told the woman. Then he just disappeared.

The woman took the suitcase home, and when she opened it, she found it was full of money. As she looked at it, she realized the money was the riches of ECK. "Now I can finally do all the things for people that I've wanted to do," she said, and very quietly she began giving away the money. She didn't need recognition for the gifts she gave because she was a humble person.

116

When she woke from the dream, the woman recognized that although she doesn't have much money in this life, she does have the true riches of ECK. She has the love of ECK, the love of the Holy Spirit. And no matter where she goes or what she does, she is able to give people what they need. They don't know it, but she's drawing from this huge suitcase that is back in a room in her dream world.

Dream Worlds Are Very Real

We know in ECK that the dream worlds are very real; they're not imagination. They are places as solid as the physical. The only difference is that most people are aware of only the physical world.

There are people in ECK who have higher states of awareness. They have the astral state of consciousness, the causal state of consciousness, even the mental state of consciousness. They are aware of life at different levels, in different heavens.

This is how it should be because this is your spiritual legacy from God to see, know, and be all that there is. And there is much more than what is here on the physical plane.

But most people are taught through science and religion that this is the extent of life. Science considers doing something again and again under lab conditions the only proof there is. So how can you prove the existence of the inner worlds? When people can't go into the inner worlds and touch that reality, they say, "The physical is all there is." Which isn't that bad for those living here, because it keeps your feet on the ground.

If you have the ability to go into the inner worlds, you can find direction there. Sometimes it comes through dreams that tell you how to live your life better. Sometimes you'll get advice about what foods to look for, for your health. Other times it even helps you in things like investments.

But don't take this information from the dream world literally without testing it.

Just because it came from the dream state, don't drop everything and run off to Alaska, for example. Test the information you get as carefully as any scientist. It may not make any sense or maybe you wouldn't want to follow it, so don't.

The Rude Saleswoman

One Saturday morning a couple decided to go shopping. There was a warehouse sale at a very expensive home-furnishings store. The sale started at ten o'clock, but next to the warehouse was the regular store which opened at nine. The couple arrived about 8:45 and saw a man outside unloading a furniture truck.

"Is there someplace nearby where we could get coffee?" they asked the man. He gave them directions to a restaurant, and they set off, but after driving around for a bit and not finding it, the couple came back to the warehouse. The young man was still unloading the truck.

He wanted to give them directions again, but they said, "No, we'll just go inside the store and wait until the warehouse opens."

As they came up to the front door of the store, a very agitated young woman greeted them. "Are you here for the warehouse sale?" she asked. "Yes," they said. "Well, you'll have to wait until ten," she said and shut the door in their faces. They opened the door and said, "Isn't this store open now?"

"Well, yes, it is," the woman said. "We'd like to look around," said the man. So the saleswoman reluctantly let them alone to wander around the store.

Just about this time, the young man from the warehouse walked up to them with two cups of coffee. "I know you didn't get your coffee, so I brought you some," he said. The couple began sipping their hot coffee as they walked around the store.

Immediately the young woman came racing out of the back room. "Coffee isn't allowed in here," she said briskly to the young man. Turning to the couple she said, "If you want to drink the coffee, you'll have to drink it outside."

It was cold outside, and the couple looked at each other. The wife told me this was normally when she and her husband would have lost their tempers and said some things to the saleswoman. But it didn't happen that time. Very kindly, the wife said to the agitated young woman, "I can understand how you feel. We also have a home with very many expensive furnishings, but we know how to drink coffee so we don't spill it all over. You can trust us that we won't do it here."

The young woman was still upset and said some rather unkind things in return. So the wife said, "I think it was bad business for you to criticize an employee in front of us. He was just trying to serve a customer, making us feel welcome." At this the young woman began to apologize.

"My dog's been sick," she said, "and I haven't slept much." Then she walked into the back room.

The couple looked around some more, then the wife saw the young woman talking in the back room with an older man. She couldn't help overhearing how worried the young woman sounded about her sick dog. She was very upset. "I don't even know if I should be at work today," she was telling the elderly man.

The wife walked over to her. "I couldn't help overhearing," she said. "I have a cat, but I used to have a dog. We love our pets as much as we would love a child."

Then the ECKist went over and hugged the saleswoman. "I have to apologize for my rude behavior," the saleswoman told her. "I just feel so bad. I guess I just have to chill out."

Then the ECKist said to her, "Well, you could have a cup of coffee and drink it outside." Fortunately, the saleswoman had gotten her sense of humor back, and they both laughed.

Showing Love

In this particular situation, the ECK wife was showing the riches of ECK, what she had gotten inwardly in love from the Holy Spirit. Instead of flying off the handle, she waited a little bit. She wasn't going to let the rude treatment of this person spoil her Saturday morning. That was her first goal. But because she kept looking, she heard more of the story, that this young woman had some problems that hurt her very much. Then the ECKist was able to give love and understanding.

Often I feel when I give these talks that they are simply a pouring back and forth of the ECK Stream, of the Holy Spirit, back and forth. Why? So that others can benefit from your experience and you can benefit from theirs.

In my position as a Wayshower, I am a go-between. In that sense, I try to pass along some of your very good experiences. May the blessings be.

ECK Springtime Seminar, Washington, D.C.,
Sunday, April 19, 1992

A person who realizes that God's hand is in everything that occurs in that person's life is someone who has a degree of spiritual freedom.

10

The Way to Spiritual Freedom

It is often a challenge to speak on Friday evenings at the ECK seminars. You've all just come from traveling. You're still mentally and emotionally going through all the airports, facing car rentals and cabs and all this. You bring it all with you.

So Friday night is generally a tough time to give a talk. By Saturday night, everybody gets more friendly. It's easier.

Getting Warmed Up

Sometimes I need to get warmed up too. This evening as I was getting cleaned up to come down here, I was shaving. I noticed that the water from the tap was ice cold. It was very uncomfortable. Then when I went to get in the shower, the water there was icy too. I let it run awhile, but it didn't get any warmer. Finally I edged in. It took my breath away.

I thought maybe it was because of the number of people in the hotel showering at the same time. But when I got out of the shower and went to the sink again, the water was warm. I didn't notice it at first because I was so cold, I was shaking. But the water gradually got hot. "This is really strange," I said.

Then I thought, *What about the shower water?* I was in a hurry, but some things you just have to know or you spend your whole life wondering. So I turned on the shower, and the water was warm! It got really hot—about three minutes after I'd gotten out of the shower!

Maybe this is when I warm up, when I start using words. I started using all kinds of words in the bathroom tonight. I got that out of my system so you'd get the cleaned-up version.

How Do You Handle Problems?

We have a pretty easy time in a number of ways. But what surprises me about people so often today is when they stub a toe in life.

Say they stub their toe at work or something. Right away it's a criminal action. They want to take it to the Supreme Court. They feel they have been done a great injustice. I shake my head and say, "If only they had seen real suffering, such as in Africa, Eastern Europe, or right here in the U.S. These people haven't suffered enough. Otherwise they wouldn't cry over a stubbed toe."

When people complain about something that doesn't really matter a whole lot, it's because they don't have much spiritual experience. Because they complain so much, it shows they are very far from spiritual freedom. Their circle of experience is too small. Some people who have never heard of ECK are farther along on the spiritual path than ECKists who complain about insignificant things.

I like a person who, when life throws them a fastball that knocks them flat, gets up and says, "Well, at least I can still get up."

Every knockdown in life is teaching you to be stronger, to stand more sturdily. Each hardship and trial is actually there as a gift from God, to make you stronger. If people understood this, they wouldn't complain so much.

I try to remember this in my own life, when the water in the shower runs cold. I try not to complain too much, but sometimes we forget.

If we complain, I think it's easier if we don't take ourselves too seriously, if we know we're just having a bad day. People can forgive that. But if you walk under a dark cloud for weeks, you rain on everyone who comes close.

Songstress

For awhile this summer, we were woken each morning by a robin with a beautiful voice. About 5:00 a.m. she would start with a song full of trills, and I would just lie there and love listening. "What a beautiful songstress," I said to my wife. It was cool enough this summer to have the windows open. "Can life get much better than this?" I asked.

After about a week or two, this beautiful bird moved off into another territory; we could hear her in the distance. Right after she left another bird settled in. He started singing early in the morning, too. His first song sounded like, "Near, near, near." About midmorning he'd change to "Peer, peer, peer." It almost sounded like "pure." But by late afternoon it was "Sneer, sneer, sneer."

"Didn't anyone ever tell that bird that he wouldn't make friends if he says, 'Sneer, sneer, sneer'?" I asked my wife.

Then I realized that this is how some people live their whole lives. Some go around saying, "Near, near," as in "Nearer my God to thee." Others say, "Peer, peer," as in "Pure in heart." But other people are always feeling the heat of life and they say, "Sneer, sneer, sneer." This is about the time I shut the window. This is also about the time other people close themselves off to the one who is always complaining.

Recognizing the Need

The way to spiritual freedom is really very easy. But first you've got to recognize that there is a need to have spiritual freedom. That's a big step. Most people never come to that in a single lifetime. It never occurs to them that they don't have spiritual freedom.

Once you come to the realization that you are without spiritual freedom, then comes the question of how you go about getting it.

In the teachings of ECK, we have a very pat answer: You do the Spiritual Exercises of ECK. The mainstay is to chant HU, an ancient name for God. You sing HU once or twice a day for ten or fifteen minutes to spiritualize your state of consciousness.

During the time you're singing HU, you are saying to Divine Spirit, "I've opened myself to you. Give me the understanding and the wisdom to meet the waves of life, and the problems, troubles, and whatever else. Give me the strength to meet life." This is basically all that we do when we do a Spiritual Exercise of ECK.

A short session where we meet with the Divine: that is a Spiritual Exercise of ECK.

Yardsticks

It's hard to say exactly what spiritual freedom is. At times it's easier to say what it is not. Sometimes when a person sees tragedy, has troubles, or finds his or her faith shaken, it causes that person to ask, "Why does God allow this to happen?" If you ask yourself that question, you would be one who does not have spiritual freedom.

If you are a person having troubles in your everyday life, you might say, "Now what purpose could there be to my having this kind of a situation at work where this person is constantly on my case, causing trouble for me? What possible reason could there be?" A person who has to ask such a question does not have spiritual freedom.

Or say people blame us for something that someone else did, and we feel we have been a victim of injustice. We ask, "Why does something like that happen to me?" We really don't understand. I think this is another indication that a person does not have spiritual freedom.

In other words, any person who cannot understand what's happening in life does not have spiritual freedom.

Seeing God's Hand in Everything

Those are the people who do not have spiritual freedom. How do we identify those who do have it? This is very hard for me to explain.

The easiest way is simply to say, "A person who realizes that God's hand is in everything that occurs in that person's life is someone who has a degree of spiritual freedom." If you look at people who are constantly unhappy, complaining, or criticizing, you'd have to say that they aren't anywhere near having spiritual freedom.

Then you find sweet people — the ones that life throws everything negative at that it can — and these people are always up. They're happy. They've had all kinds of losses and troubles, but if you met them in the store or on the street, you'd never guess.

One Step Forward

These are people who have a degree of spiritual freedom. They can see, to some degree, that whatever is happening to them is a part of the spiritual plan. It's a part of their spiritual unfoldment.

You'll often hear people like this say, "I don't understand why this happened to me, but I know it's for the good. In some way, it's for the good." This is a step.

It's a better, or higher, step than someone who falls into the Dark Night of Soul when things happen and asks, "Why did this happen to me? Is God a loving God, or is God not a loving God?"

The question is Where is spiritual freedom?

Most of us, if we had it, wouldn't recognize it. And if we don't recognize it, what good is it?

Circles of Activity

Everybody has access to spiritual freedom. But here's the funny thing: Having it is one thing, but realizing it is necessary before you can enjoy the fruits of it.

This is what we are all about in ECKANKAR. To realize the gifts of God and Divine Spirit. To realize what we already have, and not do it in an abstract way. To realize that every event in your life is a small circle of activity that fits into a larger circle, and into yet larger circles.

Life is a series of circles of activity.

You are at the center of your universe, and very close to you are other circles. Your mate is a circle of activity that is very close to you, as are your children, parents, friends, and other loved ones. These are all circles of Souls around you. And some are far from you. The world is full of Souls.

Astronomers have recently found there are other stars that have solar systems very similar to ours. We knew it in a general way before, but now we have the possibility of life being in other places besides earth. Someday it'll be a very natural fact in earth history and science. And these beings will probably be as strange to us as the people of the Soviet Union were several years ago. Why? Because their habits and their way of approaching life were so different from our own. We had very little in common.

Every area has its circle, or state, of consciousness. People within that circle are fairly comfortable with others within that circle, but not with those outside of their circle of knowledge or experience.

So the perimeters of these circles become borders. And on top of the borders of these walls we put barbed wire and hate—almost a sure sign there is no freedom. And if there is no freedom, there certainly is no spiritual freedom underlying any kind of material, or emotional, or mental freedom. Because spiritual freedom underlies all freedom.

Understanding Another's Truth

Sometimes I wonder how to explain truth, or Divine Spirit, or any of these principles of life to someone who doesn't know ECKANKAR terms. Because every religious, scientific, or philosophical group has their own special way of speaking.

This is certainly true in the computer world. To an outsider, it's pure jumble. At first you cannot understand what the people in that circle are speaking about, but as you become a member and you read more about that area of interest, you begin to understand.

There are some writers who are very skilled at bridging the gap. Many of you have computers today. We forget that ten years ago computers were more rare than calculators. But we take them for granted now. They've become part of our lives, and we don't think twice about them.

You Can't Follow Two Masters

I recommend that a person study the teachings of ECK for two years, then decide if there is an inner nudge to become a member of ECK or follow another path. The saying is that you cannot have two masters. You cannot follow two branches of truth. If you try, the price is very great. It takes a toll.

Yet I want to emphasize that I say this in an advisory capacity. It's for your own information. You can make your life a lot easier if you understand the principle that no one can have two masters. But there isn't a cutoff at two years or three years or four years.

And the cutoff generally isn't something that is brought to bear out here. For instance, after two or three years I don't come to somebody and say, "Now you have to make a decision. You have to become a member of ECKANKAR or go back to your own path." I cannot do that. This has to come from inside you. But I'm telling you out here how it works.

Almost everyone in ECKANKAR today at one time belonged to another group. I can say this because ECKANKAR didn't come into the public before 1965. The people in ECK come from all religions on earth. And somewhere along the line, something happened to those of you who are now in ECKANKAR and you found you didn't fit in the teachings you used to belong to.

The reason you went looking elsewhere is because that religion didn't answer the questions you had about spiritual freedom and truth and other questions you had. If it had, why would you have gone looking elsewhere? But you did go looking elsewhere. And as you looked, you found ECKANKAR.

A Natural Transition to ECK

A lot of people who come to ECKANKAR remain in their original church for two or three years. In fact, in the early days of ECKANKAR some of the Higher Initiates still belonged to churches. Paul Twitchell, the modern-day founder of ECKANKAR, allowed people to stay in their churches and be members of ECKANKAR because he knew they would eventually outgrow one teaching or the other. They would very naturally go where they felt most comfortable.

And this is how it is in ECK today. One day you look around and suddenly realize that you're no longer a member of the group you came from. That your heart is with ECK, the teachings of Divine Spirit. It is suddenly very natural for you.

You will have a new insight into life. You will hardly be able to think of yourself as you were before. You will know and understand things because you have had personal experience in the worlds of God beyond the physical plane.

Spiritual Experience

The basis for the teachings of ECK is experience, spiritual experience. Often the person who comes to ECK finds the change that takes place occurs initially in the dream state. Sometimes these early dreams are just a mishmash of experiences; they don't make any sense. You say, "I don't understand these dreams at all." Then it occurs to you that you are remembering dreams whereas you never used to.

It's a step. You are becoming more aware of yourself as a person operating in a greater spiritual sphere.

Some of you are fortunate to have a more aware or more conscious experience in the other worlds; we call this Soul Travel. It simply means that you are awakening in the other worlds and having an experience there with the Light and Sound of God or the ECK Masters.

When you wake up, you bring back more love and greater understanding about yourself that you never realized existed. Yet you can't tell anyone about it. You can try, and most people do. But you find out that unless others have had that experience, no one knows what you're talking about.

Where Is That Light?

A woman heard about ECKANKAR back in 1983 from her boyfriend, but she didn't have much interest in it. She had come from a strong Christian family; her father was a minister. Her mother would get the kids up at 5:30 a.m. for prayer. At 9:00 p.m. they would study the Bible and pray again. For them, just about everything they needed in life was handled through prayer.

Well, between 1983 and 1989, her brother became very ill, terminally ill. Near the end he began to speak of this marvelous light that had come to him.

Today there is much public information about people who have near-death experiences. They go through a tunnel and see this light, but they still don't know how to tie it all together. What does this light mean?

Scientists who study this make guesses. They say it may be an emotional thing. But the man said, "This is so beautiful. I can't even put it into words." He never spoke of the Sound; he didn't get to that aspect.

When his mother heard him, she said, "Pray to Jesus to heal you."

"Why, he's right here, Mother," the dying man replied. "He's sitting in that chair. He's the man who comes and takes me into the other worlds to see this bright light. It's brighter than the sun here on earth." The man told her that if he ever recovered, he would look and look until he found information about this beautiful light he saw in his dreams. But the man died shortly after that.

There are many masters working on the inner planes who deal with the higher aspects of the Holy Spirit, the Light and Sound. Many of them know about the Light, but not all of these know about the Sound of God. One of the few examples in the Bible that mentions both the Light and Sound of the Holy Spirit is the story of Pentecost where there were tongues of fire and the sound of rushing wind.

Finding Proof

After her brother died, the woman became somewhat disenchanted with her religion. She was still praying because she had been doing that since childhood and the teachings were as close as her mother's hug. But soon she came to a crossroads in her life. She had learned about ECKANKAR, and she knew she couldn't follow two paths at the same time. She had to make a decision.

So she said in contemplation, "If there really is a Mahanta, come to me and prove yourself." And she began to sing HU, this ancient name for God.

Suddenly in her inner vision, the woman saw what looked like the flame of a candle. The light of the flame began to grow larger and larger until the Mahanta stepped from the center of it. He was dressed in a very light color of yellow, which signified the Soul Plane. This was proof to her that the Mahanta was real.

133

Stages of Spiritual Growth

The higher you go into the God Worlds, the brighter the light. The Soul Plane is the Fifth Plane; on the Sixth Plane the color is an even lighter yellow. It gets lighter and brighter the higher you go until it becomes the pure, blinding white Light of God.

There are many stages before that. A person first must become a master of the physical plane, here on earth. That is the First Initiation, which comes during the dream state. Every member of ECKANKAR gets it; some remember, some don't.

After two years of outer study as a member of ECKANKAR, a person can receive the Second Initiation. This is both an outer and an inner initiation. Sometimes the inner initiation comes first, sometimes it comes later. You meet in a brief ceremony with an ECK Initiator, who is working as a representative of the Mahanta, the Living ECK Master to give you a linkup with Divine Spirit, the Light and Sound of God. From then on, your life begins to change.

Holy Moment

An initiation is a most holy moment. Not only does the person getting the initiation walk into the presence of the Divine Spirit, but also the Initiator. Both are standing in the circle of Divine Spirit more so than they do ordinarily. A lot of people just aren't aware of it. But during the time of initiation, people open their awareness and recognize the linkup with Divine Spirit.

Sometimes the awareness of this linkup comes in a gentle way, like a dream. Sometimes it comes later, when you wake up one morning with a feeling of love and wholeness you've never felt before. It begins to change you in little ways. Little by little, your Spiritual Eye opens and your heart opens to love.

Your heart opens to love because the teachings of ECK are about receiving God's love. When you begin receiving God's love, that is the way to spiritual freedom.

And the way is through HU, the love song to God.

Why Tell Stories?

As I speak, the words you hear out here are not the important thing. I always try to pick stories or a subject that has some spiritual enlightenment for you. Stories have a way of carrying longer. They're something you can take home, like a memento of the seminar.

A story has a life of its own. That's why I use them. A story will pop into your mind later, sometimes weeks later, and you'll remember it. The story then triggers the spiritual meaning behind the story. You may also recall some dreams you've had since then that tie in with the story. And you will find your life becomes holistic in a spiritual way, in a way you never before dreamed possible.

ECK Summer Festival, Anaheim, California,
Saturday, June 13, 1992

All of a suddden Peanut ran around the room. And in the middle of the room, he jumped straight up in the air. He was showing his joy at this sense of freedom.

11

Peanut's Hard Road to Freedom

There are many reasons for coming to an ECK seminar. Many of them are opportunities for inner, spiritual growth. But part of this spiritual growth is centered in meetings with friends who share the same beliefs and ideals as you. And these people come from all over the world.

The ECK seminar is an opportunity to enjoy each other's company and to cement spiritual bonds.

Inner Travels

Last night I was trying to define spiritual freedom— what it is or is not. There are three elements to gaining spiritual freedom that I want to talk about this morning. In doing this, I will refer to some of the inner travels I do.

Someone asked me a while ago, "What happens in your dreams?"

"I used to call them dreams," I said, "but now I mostly call them Soul journeys. They aren't dreams the way I used to know dreams. I am there; I am in other worlds."

Other initiates in ECK have also noticed the same thing. They'll have an experience, and they'll say, "It wasn't

137

a dream. I was there. I could see things. I could smell things. And I did things. I remember everything."

Once you can remember your journeys to the other worlds, you can learn from the lessons that occur there. You can bring them back here and gain from them spiritually.

During your physical, waking life you're not even aware most of the time, because so many things are going on. Problems catch you up in the moment so that you don't really have time to think about what it all means to you spiritually. What does this experience mean? How does it fit in? Often you're too excited or upset to put things into spiritual perspective.

But once you begin traveling into the inner worlds and having experiences which are as real as waking life, you can profit from them. You can grow spiritually from them.

The Old Red Bicycle

I'd like to give examples of three elements of spiritual freedom. You pretty much have to try to hold on to these elements as much as you can in this world.

The first involves the story of the old red bicycle. I was down by the ocean walking through a very shabby area in the inner worlds. It wasn't the pretty shoreline you would expect if I were talking about the Ocean of Love and Mercy. Then you'd expect beautiful sandy beaches, a sunny sky, and no clouds. But I wasn't in the high God Worlds on this particular journey. It was a very rugged area.

Ahead of me walked two teenagers, two young men. They were going down to the waterfront too.

As we got closer to the sea, the path we walked on had weeds growing along the side. There were people coming up the path and going down the path, back and forth. And these two young men were sometimes ahead of me, sometimes behind me.

Conditions were really bad on the waterfront itself. There were hoboes, alcoholics, and other people. In places, there were even people who had passed on, but nobody had come along to collect the empty shells yet.

The two young men were shocked, but I had seen these things before.

One of the two teenagers got on his bicycle, an old red Schwinn. That was the Cadillac of bicycles when I grew up. The boy had evidently had it since he was very young. Somewhere along the line, he had gotten tired of the color red. He had taken some white house paint and a brush and had tried to paint the bike white. But you know what it looks like when somebody tries to paint a car white with a brush. It looks like somebody tried to paint a car white with a brush.

There was a steep hill leading away from the waterfront up to a suburban area. The one boy began peddling his bicycle up this hill. The other boy had walked away, gone somewhere else. The hill was so steep, sometimes the boy was riding his bicycle, sometimes he had to get off and push it. I was just walking up the hill, yet I was able to stay pretty close to him.

When we got up to the top of the hill, I caught up with the boy. There was cross traffic. Cars were going back and forth. We had to stop. And I said, "Nice bike." I saw that underneath the paint it was a sturdy bike.

He said, "It's for sale."

I always like to encourage people, so I said, "I'll give you twenty dollars for it."

It was a very old, beat-up bike. But it looked solid, and he had no more use for it. My offer was about fifteen more dollars than he was going to get for it anywhere else.

So he said, "OK. Come over to my place. My folks are home, and we can finish this. Then you can have the bicycle. We'll finish doing what we need to."

Keeping Your Word

So I went over to his place. I stood in his living room while he went to talk with his mother. He told her he'd found someone to buy his bicycle for twenty dollars. Then she told him how to drive a hard bargain.

When he came back, I held out the twenty dollars. But he went over to the bike and started to take off the basket and the light.

I said, "What are you doing?"

He said, "They're extra."

I said, "No, our deal was twenty dollars for the thing as it stands there."

But he just kept taking off the light. He had taken the basket off by this time. I said, "No deal."

He said, "What?"

I said, "We had a deal. Twenty dollars is more than you're going to get for this bike anywhere else. I was trying to do you a favor, and now you try to make a few more dollars somewhere else and cheat me in the bargain." I said, "No deal."

His mother came running out. She tried to make everything right. "We'll put everything back on," she said. "You can have the bike for twenty."

But I said, "I don't want it. I don't need the bicycle. It would probably have made my day a little easier because I've got a long way to walk today. But I don't mind walking, and I don't need people's material things. All I wanted to do was pass the time in conversation and encourage you to do something with something that you no longer had any use for. I would have found a way to give the bicycle to someone else."

The young man tried everything to open up the deal again.

"You went back on your word," I said. "You gave your word and broke it. You can't do that. We had a deal, and we were both keeping it in good faith until you tried to renege. That's where you went wrong. You and I had an understanding."

He came after me. He didn't cry, but he was pleading. He was too old to cry. He was a teenager.

I felt bad; I wanted to give him the money anyway. But I realized that to do it wouldn't have helped him spiritually. He wouldn't have learned the lesson.

Learning from Experts

So I went down into another part of town, away from this suburban area into a manufacturing area. Two young boys came running after me. They were about ten or eleven; they hadn't hit the teen years yet. They were just wandering the streets.

They asked, "Can we come along with you?"

I said, "Sure."

We came to the warehouse I was going to. It was huge. It was big enough to hold the Goodyear blimp.

We went in a side door. The two young boys walked in, looked around, and began to jump around with joy because they sensed the freedom in this place.

When they finally settled down, I said to them, "Do you know why you have this sense of freedom?"

They shook their heads; they didn't know.

"Look at the people in here," I said.

For the first time, they looked around. The entire building was filled with craftsmen, people who were experts in their field: master carpenters, master plumbers, computer operators, designers, and interior designers. They were both remodeling this warehouse and at the same time creating products for other people.

"Look at these people," I said. "Each person here is an expert in his field. He or she can come here to practice their craft, to do whatever they do better than anyone else. They get their satisfaction from doing a job well. Buyers come here expecting the very finest, and they get it."

I said, "When you walked into this room, you had a sense of freedom. These people are living spiritual freedom. And the first step to attaining this freedom is learning how to do something well.

"They're doing this because they love it," I said, "not just because they're being paid for it. Each one of them is going to keep at it until they get so good that they naturally outgrow this particular talent. Then they'll go on to another area."

Becoming a Master Craftsman

Just then, a young man in his midtwenties came by. He said, "I overheard you talking about what it takes to attain mastership and spiritual freedom. What did you do when you worked in a production phase like this?"

I said, "I worked in printing. But whether it's printing or some other thing, you're learning how to be careful and exact with whatever you do. You're doing it for the love of God and not for the love of money. Once you go past this stage, then you're ready for the next, which is true spiritual freedom, or a greater degree of spiritual freedom."

These people already had it. So I told the two young boys, "You'll do well to come back here again tomorrow; watch what these people do. And if you care enough about what they're doing, they may show you some of the secrets of how to become a master in each one of these areas."

Self-Sufficiency

I told them to study and observe, and then they would learn. So many people today have a feeling—because life is easy, especially here in the U.S.—that you can have whatever you want just because you ask for it.

Actually, you can't. You have to earn it.

People forget this; they don't like to hear it. They'd like the government to give handouts. They like handouts because they're afraid to go outside of this little box that they have created for themselves and which makes them miserable. They always have to wait for a handout from someone else. They can never become self-sufficient.

And they are Soul. They have the infinite ability to tap into this creative fountain of life called the ECK, or Divine Spirit, and change their life.

They can do this. But they've been told that they have to work a forty-hour week, or a thirty-five-hour week. So they feel that if they work one minute more, that somehow somebody's getting the best of them.

Doing Something for Love

Nobody ever gets the best of you if you're doing something for love.

And if you're not doing it for love, you'd be better off finding something that you could do for love. Because you're not growing unless you're doing something for God.

If you're not doing something for God—or SUGMAD, as we call God in ECKANKAR—if you're not doing it for the highest principle, then there's no point in doing it. You're just getting by. And mastership is anything except getting by. You do everything until it sings.

And why? Because you want to. You love to.

The lesson of the warehouse—and the spirit of freedom that the two young boys felt—was to become an expert in something. Because you need to be grounded in something. This earth is no mistake; there is a reason to be here. There is a reason you are where you are.

Spelling Test

I left the warehouse, and the boys stayed there. I walked down several other streets and came to the town center. I went to the town center because I wanted to apply for a business license.

To get the license, I needed to take some tests. I went into a little room. There was a table with three other people seated around it. An old judge was administering the tests. In his hand he held the licenses. But before he signed the papers to give us the right to work and to be part of the town's community, he said, "I've given you several tests, but here's the last one. It's a spelling test."

I thought, *That's kind of strange, a spelling test.* But since I was good at spelling, I thought, *No problem.*

It was only a ten-word test. But the table was cluttered with papers—my papers and the papers of the other three people. As the old judge gave the first spelling word, I pulled a piece of paper toward me. It was full of writing, but near the top there were a couple of empty lines going sideways. *I'll just write up here,* I thought.

But it didn't look neat enough. I wanted to put the

words in columns because that's how I was used to doing it in grade school and high school. So I looked around.

It took him about ten seconds before he had another word for us to spell. *I'll look for another piece of paper and then copy these down,* I thought. But as I looked for another piece of paper, he came and took my first paper away. Now I had to remember the words—he was up to the third word already. I had to remember these words and look for a clean piece of paper. As soon as I had written them down, one of the other people took away that paper.

The judge came up with a word like *sylph*. This means an elemental creature of the air, a graceful woman or young girl.

Another spelling word was simple, like *room*. He gave all different kinds of words. He wanted to find out the range of a person's ability from the highest to the lowest. Because to do business in that town, you had to have the ability to read and write. This way, he was able to test your ability to wade through the government forms. There was some kind of reasoning behind his test.

But finally I said, "I don't like these conditions." And so I left.

What's the Lesson?

Spelling was a skill. I was good at it, totally confident. But I was trying to remember all these words, write them on different pieces of paper, and keep everything lined up.

When people started to take the paper I'd written all this on, I realized this is often what happens when a person moves forward spiritually, as you will notice in your own life. Other people will do things to make it hard for you.

This doesn't mean we blame them. But sometimes you just notice what people are doing. You say, "OK, maybe I had this coming. But I'm not sure how much of it I'm going to stand for before I change the circumstances and get myself out of here. If I can't get those people to leave me alone, then I'm going to leave and not put up with it." This is another way of dealing with it too. It's not the chicken's way out. Sometimes it's the only way to keep or maintain your spiritual freedom.

With the old, red bicycle, the lesson was: Keep your word.

In the warehouse where the spirit of freedom was, it was: Become an expert in something.

The spelling test and the interference by the judge and the others so that I couldn't take the test gave this lesson: Others will try to hold you back whenever they can if they see you're advancing spiritually. For instance, they will tell you all kinds of reasons why you should not follow ECKANKAR.

Turning Point

I got much of this thrown at me, as I know some of you have. People will throw all kinds of fear at you. Sometimes I just trembled. But yet, inwardly, I was moving toward a teaching that would give me more freedom and more love than I had ever had before. A tension between the old teachings and the new teachings grew within me. And somewhere, sometime, I had to make a decision and say, "It is one or the other."

Sometimes we find it easier to take the comfortable way. We say, "I'm going to go back the way I was." There's nothing wrong with it.

It simply means we haven't the strength to go forward and accept the love that the ECK, or Divine Spirit, is offering us. Unless you are strong, you won't be able to accept the love that God or the Holy Spirit showers upon you. The weak cannot stand the love of God. I know this is a shocking statement, but it's true.

Only the strong can stand the true love of God.

This is why in ECKANKAR we realize that no matter what comes up in life, we must find a way to deal with it. We have to make our choices.

Oddly enough, the choices we make are neither right nor wrong. They are simply our choices. Each choice is based upon our strength and perception, at the moment, of what truth means to us. Does it mean a lot? Does it mean a little? How badly do we desire divine love? How badly do we desire God?

Desire for God

Some people desire God more, and they will let nothing stand between them and the highest consciousness. Other people say they desire the highest truth, but if the smallest thing comes along on the path to God, they trip and fall off. And they're very happy to sit in the ditch and go home after they get up. And it's OK. It doesn't matter.

We have all stubbed our toes on the path to God. We have all fallen in the ditch. We have all turned around and gone home, back to our material home, not home to God. We've gone back where we came from.

Back where we came from is the place of our unhappiness, the reason we started walking the path to God in the first place. The old life didn't fulfill our needs, and so we began to look farther. We began to look beyond the horizon of our backyard, saying, "There must be something more. Where is it? Dear God, let me find it."

147

When God let you find it, you found out that maybe you weren't ready to walk the path home to God. It takes the very strong to accept the love of God.

Peanut's Hard Road to Freedom

Peanut, a rabbit, belongs to one of the ECK members. This ECKist had been given the rabbit by somebody who asked, "Do you want a one-and-a-half-year-old rabbit?"

She said, "Sure."

This ECKist hadn't had a rabbit since she was a child, and she thought it would be really nice to have one for a pet.

In American Indian lore, a rabbit is the epitome of fear. There's nothing quite as afraid of life as a rabbit, because it really has nothing to defend itself with. It has no sharp teeth. It can put up a fight, but it doesn't have natural defenses except speed. So the rabbit has to take advantage of speed.

Well, the ECKist brought the rabbit home. He sat in his cage all the first day. He came in a steel cage that clipped over a two-foot square bottom pan.

The second day when the woman took the cage top off to clean the pan, the rabbit just sat in the pan. He wouldn't leave, although he could have free run of the kitchen. Suddenly she got a certain feeling from the rabbit: The name Peanut came. She said, "I guess your name is Peanut."

After that she called him Peanut. He was a little brown rabbit, and he didn't really want to jump around the kitchen. So she took him up to the bedroom and set him down there. And Peanut moved very carefully around the room, testing this new freedom. Until now, he had known only his little cage. There's not too much freedom in a cage.

All of a sudden Peanut ran around the room. And in the middle of the room, he jumped straight up in the air. It was his joy at this sense of freedom.

The ECKist was so happy for Peanut. She said, "Little Peanut has freedom and now knows joy."

She spent a few days sitting in her bedroom, reading a book and watching the rabbit. The rabbit would come over to her sometimes. Then she found out that rabbits like to eat paper and wood. And she also found she wasn't getting some of her other work done. She thought it would work out a little better if she took Peanut down to the kitchen.

So she took the cage down to the kitchen and opened it. She expected the explosion of brown rabbit. She thought Peanut would pop right out of that cage and go running around the kitchen. But Peanut sat in the cage. He wouldn't move, wouldn't budge.

She tried everything. She brought a little rug over and set him on the rug. But as soon as she let go of him, Peanut hopped right back in the cage. She'd take him out and set him on the rug again, and Peanut would hop back into the cage. She was trying to let him know, "You can run around the kitchen." She had the kitchen door blocked off so that he couldn't get into the other areas of the home.

All Peanut would do was stick his nose over the edge of the pan and just sniff. One day, he did a little hop to the rug, then went right back into the cage. Back and forth just a little bit.

Trying Out New Freedom

This isn't going real well, the ECKist thought. She had a spare room she was going to clean and paint. *Maybe we can spend more time together in there,* she thought.

It was kind of neutral ground between the kitchen and the bedroom. The room was right across from her bedroom, and the rabbit seemed to get along OK there. After a while, she opened the door to let Peanut have the run of the house, but he would stop, just as if he had run into an electric fence. He would come right up to the doorway and stop. But Peanut wouldn't go through the door. Rabbit, again, is fear.

The ECKist didn't know what to do. She said, "I've tried to pull the rabbit out of his cage. He won't come. I've tried to pull him out of his room. He won't come. So I'll try to coax him."

She lay down in the doorway of the bedroom across from this third room and said, "Come on, Peanut. Come on, Peanut. You can do it!" All the rabbit had to do was hop out of the room and into the hallway.

Peanut wanted to come, but he didn't have the courage. One day, he finally got all his courage together. Peanut ran from that third room into the bedroom, ran around it a few times, ran back out in the hallway, and ran around there a couple times. Pretty soon, Peanut had the freedom to run in this third room and the bedroom and the hallway, just back and forth. And Peanut felt really good.

By the time she had written this letter to me, the ECKist said Peanut had the run of the house. In other words, Peanut had overcome his fear and could run throughout the house.

We Have Fear Too

The ECKist realized she was very much like Peanut. When she had first come into ECKANKAR, the Mahanta had taken her out of the cage, which was her own little world. He had taken the top off and said to her, "Here, you're free. You can run around in this bigger room." But she was afraid and didn't want to step out of her own comfortable little world.

Gradually, the Mahanta tried to show her there was nothing to fear, that there was a greater room and a greater world outside.

Trying to pull Peanut out of the cage didn't work, any more than it did for the Master to take the ECKist out in the dream state. So finally the Master just coaxed and encouraged her. And she was able to accept the greater spiritual freedom that she found in ECKANKAR, not just in the teachings, but in the other worlds. These other worlds are the heavens of God. This is why they are so important to us.

Writing to the Master

I would like to give one spiritual exercise before you go. So often, people say, "I simply cannot deal with my life. Everything is wrong. I can't get over this problem."

Sit down and write an initiate report. Or if you're not an initiate, a personal letter to the Master. You don't have to mail it. Now this is important: When you're feeling very upset and down on the world, when you don't have the confidence you want or you're feeling at odds with people, this is the time to sit down somewhere and write an initiate report. You don't have to mail them, as I said.

I'm emphasizing this because you'll find that the Mahanta works inwardly with each person. You don't have to understand how it works because that isn't important.

All you have to understand is whether it works for you. If it works for you, that's all that matters because your spiritual unfoldment is at stake here. Your spiritual freedom and your greater sense of receiving divine love.

First, write down very clearly what's bothering you. Do this in the first or second paragraph. Even the first or second sentence if you can. Say, "This is what's troubling me. I can't handle it." Then keep writing some of the experiences that have happened that support the problem you're having. Say, "I'm having this certain problem with somebody at work. And here are some of the things that this person has done to me."

Write it down. And as you write, after about five, ten, or fifteen minutes, you're going to find that something's lifting from you. You will definitely feel something lifting.

If it's a really bad problem, you may have to write for fifteen or twenty minutes, not just five or ten. You'll feel something lifting. The problem won't be as heavy as it was before. And if this feeling of depression comes back again— in a day or two, a week, or a month—sit down and write about it again. This requires self-discipline.

This is one of the steps to self-mastery: learning how to have the discipline to very directly face what's causing you trouble.

Put it down on a piece of paper in the first two sentences. Put in the details. You can do this with a tape recorder too. It doesn't make any difference. Just get it out. Sometimes this will be much more beneficial than seeking professional help.

Healing Problems from Long Ago

There's a place for professional counseling. There is. But when you're working with the Mahanta, he can go beyond birth.

You don't have to worry about childhood traumas. People who worry about childhood traumas forget that everybody comes into this life with a debt. This is responsible for the childhood trauma, not some human being who happened to be thrown into this situation with you in your childhood. That's too shallow.

Any kind of healing that can only go back to your childhood or your birth is a superficial kind of healing. I'm not saying there isn't a place for it. For instance, if you have a toothache, go to a dentist. If you have another medical ailment, go to a doctor. If you can't see well, go to an eye doctor of some sort.

Why? Because you have an immediate physical problem.

But in some of these things, there's a karmic cause way back. Some things you just have to live with, like maybe poor eyesight. But other things you don't have to live with. But you need help that takes you back beyond your childhood.

Unwinding Your Karma

If you give this over to the Mahanta in an initiate report, he can take you back in the dream state and begin unwinding this karma.

No one else can do that for you.

This is when you're going to be unwinding the real cause of the serious problems that are making you the flawed spiritual being that you are today, but which you do not have to remain.

With this, I would like to conclude this talk on spiritual freedom and wish you well on your way home and on your journey home to God. May the blessings be.

ECK Summer Festival, Anaheim, California,
Sunday, June 14, 1992

153

The ECK, or Holy Spirit, provides the bricks and mortar, but it's up to you whether you use them as stumbling blocks or as stepping-stones.

12

What Is Spiritual Freedom?

Spiritual freedom is a difficult topic to talk about, because in the grand view of things, spiritual freedom means to be free of whatever is causing us problems here.

Most people have problems of a kind that make them bitter, angry, and fearful. But if someone were to say to them, "Would you like spiritual freedom, even if it meant leaving this earth permanently?" most would hedge. They're not eager for such a thing. They want it later, maybe when they're 105 or something.

The ultimate state of spiritual freedom brings wisdom, love, and spiritual power. But there are stages in between. We expand or unfold from no freedom into a greater state of spiritual freedom.

Stumbling Blocks or Stepping-Stones?

The ECK, or Holy Spirit, provides the bricks and mortar. I'm here to point them out to you, to say, "Those are the bricks, and there's the mortar." Most people don't recognize them.

And what are you going to do with them?

155

The Holy Spirit provides them, somebody points them out to you, but it's up to you whether you use them as stumbling blocks or as stepping-stones.

There's a trend today in society. A person will take the mortar and slop it on the ground where it hardens into big clumps. It has sharp edges, and the person trips on it but always says, "It's somebody else's fault." To me, this is such a waste of spiritual potential.

Creative Ability Is Survival

What does it mean to be a spiritual being?

It means to employ the highest force of creativity that is possible among people. Creative power means figuring your way out of a situation once you get yourself into it. Because most of the time we find ourselves in trouble that we've made ourselves.

The definition of someone with the golden heart is someone who lives in the presence of God, in the spirit of love.

That means you pay more attention to the needs of other people than to your own. It doesn't mean neglecting your own needs, of course; a person who is unable to take care of himself or herself certainly isn't going to be able to help anyone else.

Until you become a strong human being—able to survive under any and all conditions—you're never going to be able to help anyone else. In ECKANKAR, we want to see people develop into strong human beings. This is a path for the strong. The meek shall inherit the earth, but the strong shall go into the highest reaches of heaven.

The Garage Door Opener

This morning I went into the bathroom, and there was a huge spider, a daddy longlegs, on my bath towel. I'd seen him under a shelf a week ago, and as long as he stayed there, I didn't care. But it might be hard on him to be on my towel; he might get crunched or we might both have a fright when I try to dry myself.

So I went downstairs and got a glass and an index card. It wasn't even a struggle getting him into the glass. I carried him to the garage and balanced the glass in one hand as I reached to push the button for the garage door opener. As I pressed the button, there was an enormous blue flash. It startled me so much I almost dropped the glass. The spider fell to the floor and scurried away.

Whenever something very startling like this happens, I know there's a spiritual lesson in it. It looked like the light had burned out on the garage door opener.

"As long as I'm here, I'll replace that burned-out lightbulb," I said to my wife. So I went back inside to get a new bulb.

I came back out, stood on a stepladder, and screwed in the new bulb. It stayed lit for about five seconds, then went out. "Oh no," I said, "we've got big problems." It looked like there was a short in the garage door opener.

"Now the door's going to be frozen in the open position and anyone can come in and steal my lawnmower or snow thrower," I told my wife. *Maybe this isn't so bad,* I thought.

After thinking about this problem and how I was going to fix it, it occurred to me to try the garage door opener again. A little skeptical, I walked over to the button and pressed it. To my surprise, the light came on immediately and the door closed.

I realized our garage door opener has a ten-minute timer. The light comes on when the door opens, then it shuts off after ten minutes. Apparently by the time I went inside and found a new bulb, nine minutes and fifty-five seconds had passed.

Seeing Past Illusion

Sometimes forces of illusion try to make us see things through a cloud. We draw the wrong conclusions, like I did when I thought the garage door opener was broken. But because I listened to the inner nudge to try once more, the illusion was broken instead.

It was interesting timing. I would have drawn the wrong conclusion; I did for a few seconds. But when it happened so suddenly, I asked, "What else could be wrong?"

A frozen garage door on a Sunday morning right before you leave the house could be a problem, unless you don't care too much about mowing the lawn or clearing snow from the driveway in winter. My wife wouldn't have minded, actually. She doesn't want me to mow the lawn or do these things.

Longer Life

We hear things like how we should have an easy life, not have too much tension. But under certain conditions, challenge is good. Maybe we live longer. There are studies done that show people who live alone live a shorter time than people who have someone else in the home. I think the constant presence of someone else's opinion about how you should live your life has staying power.

It's good to live longer if we are still working on achieving the steps toward spiritual freedom. That way we can learn the lessons that we would otherwise not get in this lifetime.

What is spiritual freedom?

Spiritual freedom is when a responsibility is removed and gives us more time to do the things we really want to do or like to do that are of a spiritual direction. In everyday terms, it's similar to what parents feel when the last teenager leaves home. Or what the teenager feels when he or she gets a driver's license. It's a degree of spiritual freedom.

Leaving the Nest

My daughter graduated from high school last year. When I heard she was going to graduate, I said, "Thank God."

If you're a parent, you can understand what I mean. If the child doesn't graduate, it's like a baby robin who doesn't leave the nest. By the end of summer, the parent robins get pretty thin from chasing around getting food for their young. Parents can run themselves ragged for their fledglings.

In a healthy family when the children are finally ready to leave home, the parents say, "Sure, I'll lend you some money to leave. Don't forget to write. And remember that eighteen is the cutoff date for unlimited financial aid."

The thought of going back to life the way it was before you had children takes awhile to soak in sometimes. Just the thought of it can give you this feeling of lightness and happiness. Yet some parents are heartbroken, seeing the home suddenly empty. What are they going to fill their lives with now? Other parents, however, are happy to go out to dinner and not have to worry about being home before dark.

Rite of Passage

When this rite of passage occurs for the child, it's a state of freedom reached by the parents too.

This is as it should be; it's basically what nature does. The only species that violates this is the human being, when children become professional beggars before their time. They hang on at home, and any parent with any sense of humanity cannot throw them out, even though it might be the best thing to do for both parent and child.

What does life require of us? To be able to survive, to go out there and have the experiences of life, and to learn from them. To become better spiritual beings.

And by becoming better spiritual beings, we become more self-sufficient. We become better able to handle ourselves in one crisis after another, as well as in the good times. This moves us toward spiritual freedom in this lifetime. When you have more spiritual freedom, you have more happiness and independence. This is what we are looking for.

My daughter went to Alaska this summer to work in a fish cannery. I strongly encouraged her, short of buying the plane ticket, which I let her earn herself. She was also earning spending money; she wanted to have two or three hundred dollars by the time she left. She said her friends would be taking ninety or one hundred dollars each. "You're going to do fine," I told her.

But I think she decided to take it easy for a few weeks before she left. She was going with six friends, and they spent a week packing things into duffel bags.

Just before she left I talked with her again on the phone. "How much money do you have?" I asked.

"About a hundred dollars," she said.

"What happened?" I asked. "You were going to have a lot more."

"Well, Dad," she said, "I had to pack."

I realized it doesn't take two weeks to pack a duffel bag, but I also wasn't going anywhere in this argument. "Call me if you need any money," I told her.

I had told her to take this adventure because if she stayed home she'd regret it for the rest of her life. She and her friends got their courage from each other. It was enough to get them to Alaska. They're out on the first of the Aleutian Islands, no trees, no brush, just sand and three or four dormitories for the students who come to process the fish. She got homesick quickly. There's no radio, no TV.

Giving Others Freedom

After my daughter had left, her mother called me. "Moonies are running that cannery," she said. She was concerned. "What if they try to change her religion?"

"I don't care," I said. "If she wants to leave ECKANKAR and become a Moonie or a Lutheran or a Catholic or a Hindu or anything, it's OK. I don't own her." I had spent the better part of eighteen years imagining the worst thing this child could ever do to me. Because if you can figure that out, the child can't control you.

A dear friend of mine who grew up a Southern Baptist raised two sons; one became a Mormon (and married one) and one became an atheist. My friend always let people enjoy their religious freedom, even at home. He didn't push his kids. He went to church, and they came along when they felt like it. He still goes to his Baptist church today, but he's busy now getting ready for a visit from his new Mormon relatives.

When Love Replaces Fear

What is spiritual freedom?

Spiritual freedom is growing into a state of more godliness. Becoming more aware of the presence of God.

161

How do you do this? By becoming aware of the lessons behind your everyday experiences. This is how you grow into a loving awareness of the presence of God.

Most people live under the hand of fear. You buy life insurance; you wear seat belts. Why? Because you're afraid of what might happen if you get into an accident.

When you get a little more spiritual freedom, love comes into your heart and replaces fear with wisdom. This is the golden heart. You start making decisions based on a greater degree of wisdom instead of fear. You say, "Maybe I'm not wearing this seat belt out of fear; I just find it a wise thing to do."

But how do you get your heart open?

The Swedish Couple and the Rock Musician

A friend from Sweden told me a story of a couple who traveled to New York City. They were unsophisticated travelers; when their friends learned where they were going, everyone warned them about crime in New York. "Don't ride the subway; watch out for cabdrivers," they said.

But the Swedish couple arrived safely and got to their hotel, even went on a few guided tours. They had a few days free, but they didn't want to leave their hotel room because of all the terrible things that could happen out there.

One day they were running short of refreshments, and since room service was too expensive for their budget, the wife decided to take her life in her hands and go to the corner store. As she got on the elevator, a huge man came in with a huge dog. The man was the leader of a rock band; he had a huge head of hair, well-worn jeans, and chains around his neck.

The woman was petrified; she stood in the corner of the elevator shaking as the doors closed. All the warnings of her friends came back to her mind. And here her worst fears had walked right into the elevator with her.

The dog was curious about the woman and moved over to her. He began sniffing her dress, as dogs do.

"Down," the rock musician commanded.

The dog got down on the floor. And the woman got down right beside him, her hands over her head.

The rock musician began to laugh. He laughed until tears streamed down his face. He was still laughing as the elevator doors opened and he walked across the lobby into the street.

The poor Swedish woman was so scared she got off the elevator on her hands and knees. Finally gathering her courage, she stood up and went to the corner store. By the time she got back to the hotel room she was too embarrassed to tell her husband what had happened.

For the next few days, every time the couple went down to the hotel dining room, the whole rock band was there. As soon as the woman walked in, the entire group started to laugh. They laughed until tears ran down their faces and they finally had to leave the dining room. The woman's husband wondered what had happened.

Mercifully, the day came when they could check out and return home to Europe, back to sanity. The couple went to the front desk to pay their large bill, but the clerk said, "Your bill's paid for. And here's a letter for the lady."

The letter was from the rock musician.

"Thank you so much," he had written. "I have never laughed so much in my whole life. But I realize we embarrassed you, and to make up for this I am paying for your hotel room. We wish you a happy journey. Thank you for the joy and laughter you brought to us."

A Gift of Laughter

This was the journey of the Swedish couple to New York City, where they learned that fear sometimes can be overcome by love. Because as the musician began to laugh, love came into his heart. It also came to the Swedish couple when he was able to give the gift of love back to the woman who had inadvertently opened his heart.

Life could not exist without either the Light or Sound of God. They show up in many different ways here in the material plane. They create the forms within which we move to get the spiritual experience we need to have spiritual freedom.

Love in Expression

One of the tour guides at the Temple of ECK was asked a question by a visitor: "Can you explain this Light and Sound in one sentence?"

No one had ever asked her to do this. She was at a loss, but she did the best she could in two or three sentences. After that she was a little nervous that someone would ask her such a question again. She wondered how to answer it.

One day she was showing someone a framed quilt downstairs in the Temple. It had a large golden €ξ in the center. She spoke about love as the creative force. Love is the force that opens your heart and allows you to experience life in fuller measure than you had before. It allows you to have more joy and appreciation for life every day.

That evening she was home hanging a picture on her wall. As she stood back to admire how nice it looked, a message came to her from the Inner Master that answered her question.

"The Light and Sound is love in expression," he said.

Love is the doorway to spiritual freedom. And the Light and Sound of God opens that doorway of love. You must go through that doorway. You must have the love of God transform your life before you can realize the gift of spiritual freedom.

Temple of ECK Worship Service, Chanhassen, Minnesota, Sunday, July 5, 1992

165

The Holy Spirit is the Voice of God, and God speaks through these two aspects of the Light and Sound. Often we take this for granted.

13

The Light and Sound
Are All Around

An ECK seminar can be a real learning experience. Like a vacation, it's time away from the routine of everyday living. Somehow we're more aware of living than usual. And I think this is good.

How We Take the Voice of God for Granted

The Holy Spirit is the Voice of God, and God speaks through these two aspects of the Light and Sound. Often we take this for granted.

In this auditorium we have the circle of light from a spotlight, the video cameras with their blinking lights. We have the sound of people coughing, of people moving, of my voice through the sound system, of the music we hear.

We take all these things for granted. But they're emanations or aspects of the Voice of God.

Visiting Paris

This is our first major seminar in Paris. We've had small seminars here in years past; we've also stayed here in Paris between the seminars in Holland and ones in

Africa. Whenever I was here, I would walk the streets of Paris, just walk everywhere. Once I even climbed the Eiffel Tower. When I came down I was really tired and hot, and it looked like as good a time as any for an ice-cream cone. I suddenly saw the wisdom of all those ice-cream carts at the base of the Eiffel Tower.

There was something about Paris I couldn't put my finger on until recently. I realized that during the day, Paris is like a flower with all its petals open. The shops are open, the little alleyways are open, the houses have their shutters open. Then at night everything closes up behind big steel doors and shutters.

Paris learned that the safest way to live in a city was to shutter the doors and windows at night. Life continues at night, but it goes on behind closed doors. It's a practical way to live with the pressures of crime and too many people.

Shutters over Soul

In a way the city itself is like so many Souls. After lifetimes of pain and fear, they shutter themselves. The light of Soul is there inside, but it's hidden by shutters upon shutters upon shutters. Outwardly, most people appear to be spiritually asleep; they've shuttered in the Light and Sound of God, and It can't get out.

In ECK we try to bring the Light and Sound of God to people through the word HU. It's an ancient love song to God, an ancient name for God. Only the Light and Sound, these two aspects of the Holy Spirit, can get through the shutters that surround Soul and open It up again so that the life within can come out. So people can leave their prisons.

We try to bring the daylight and the Sound of God into the dark worlds of Soul. So that Soul can find Itself and realize that It is a spark of God. That It need not live in darkness but can move into the light.

Our Own Efforts

Certain countries like Mexico and Singapore hold promise right now of becoming as great as Japan in the world economy. This is good for the people who've lived at the bottom of the ladder. There's a light shining over Mexico right now. Perhaps if they can keep their self-discipline—and not lose it as we have as a people in the United States—the country has a chance to become a rising star, where the people can enjoy the spiritual aspects of life as much as people from other nations do.

People all over the world are walking around in their little shuttered prisons wondering, *Is this all life has to offer?* The answer is no. It has a lot more to offer, but it takes wisdom and self-discipline to know which direction to go.

Self-discipline is a word that is hard for us to understand. Basically it means that the entitlements we expect from life are to come from our own efforts, not the hands of other people.

Dangers of Social Welfare

In the United States the government has spent an enormous amount on social reform and aid, even during this last administration. Social welfare has nearly gotten out of hand; it'll probably get a lot worse. As this happens, taxes increase. It's harder for businesses to hire employees. Then we find the unemployment rate rises, fewer people can pay taxes, and more people live in poverty.

169

Once this cycle begins, you have people voting in officials who promise them something for nothing, entitlements taken from someone else. Once that starts, it's a long slide to the bottom.

You kill yourself by taking self-responsibility away from people. It's against spiritual law. There's nothing wrong with helping people who need it, but after a while it goes far beyond this. Graft and corruption among political leaders and those who support them is then supported by people who live off the money of others. Politicians live off the votes of the poor, who are living on welfare. And the cycle never ends.

When this happens a country goes into a decline. No one has the backbone to say, "We've got to learn to stand on our own two feet again."

I'm not speaking about people who have handicaps or the elderly; I'm speaking about people who are weak in the sense of not being willing—and finally not being able—to support themselves. Even people who want to work cannot find work, because the cycle has gone out of control.

Holiday Cycles

It's like someone who gorges around the holidays instead of watching his diet. I find many people get the flu about two weeks after Thanksgiving, Christmas, or Easter. People have broken the regular habits of what they're used to eating, and their bodies can't take the overload.

But what's the easiest thing to do? Blame the flu. You blame someone or something else because this way when the next holiday comes, you're not responsible if you get sick again.

Taking Responsibility as a Nation

People in the U.S. have very little confidence in their politicians, yet the politicians reflect those who voted them into office.

When people can but won't take responsibility for their lives, they are going backward spiritually. And when a group does this as a nation, the whole country slides backward. It's a very sad thing, and it doesn't have to be this way.

But to turn it around requires self-discipline at the very bottom of the ladder, from the people.

Each of us has a certain amount of talent and skills, things we do better than anyone else. Our purpose in this life is to be a Co-worker with God. That means the hardships and lessons of everyday living are only to help us become better at what we are. So that we can see the building blocks that life has put around us.

So often people complain. "Life is so hard," they'll say, or "I'd be so much better off if so-and-so weren't around." But, again, this is not taking responsibility. Because as Soul you have access to the unlimited creative power of the Holy Spirit.

Opening the Shutters

You have to know how to open the shutters around you that make your prison dark and cold. All I can offer you is the word *HU*. This is the beginning in ECK.

They had an enormous screen on stage this morning for a slide show. I was thinking that life is nothing more than this enormous screen and our thoughts and feelings are images on the screen. They have meaning, but only according to our spiritual insight. What can we see? Will we walk into the screen and become part of life? Or will the screen remain only a white thing hanging from the ceiling? That's nothing more than living life secondhand.

In ECK, I'm trying to show you how to see that your stumbling blocks are stepping-stones.

Two Miracles

In Mexico City there was a regional ECK seminar. One of the ECKists there said she noticed how the members of ECK were working well together for the first time. Many new people came to the ECK seminar, and the room was very full of chelas. So one by one, the chelas stood up to let the newcomers have their seats.

In this small act of giving, the ECKists were recognizing these people had come to hear more about truth, as they had once done. They wanted the wisdom of God.

One of the woman there had a teenage daughter who was having trouble adjusting to life. Several times, in fact, she had tried to kill herself. This had caused much pain in the family. The mother invited her daughter to come to this seminar, and the young girl listened to the stories of other people who had some evidence of the Light and Sound in their lives.

As she sat there, her eyes grew wider. After the seminar, the young girl told her mother, "I have found my religion. I am an ECKist." The mother was so happy that her daughter had found this chance to turn her life around.

After the seminar, the woman was at home telling her neighbor about the seminar when the telephone rang. Without thinking, she picked up the receiver and held it to her left ear. When she hung up the phone, she realized that she could once again hear in that ear. The doctors had told her long ago that she'd never hear with that ear again because the nerves were dead.

The woman said to her neighbor, "Two miracles happened this weekend. My daughter found ECK, and I can hear a little in this ear again." These are the little miracles of ECK in the Light and Sound of God.

A Gift of Healing

Not everyone gets healings when they go to an ECK seminar. But some people do. Others do but don't recognize the blessings they receive. For others it takes a week or two before they look back and realize perhaps they've had a gift of healing. Perhaps something changed at work which made their lives better.

But it depends upon the individual. How conscious are you? How soon will you recognize that the stumbling blocks lying at your feet are really stepping-stones?

You can open yourself and gain a greater awareness of who and what you are as Soul. You can do this by singing HU. Sing it to yourself, or sing it out loud. But do it every day.

HU—Your Key to Secret Worlds

HU is your key to your secret worlds. Once you learn to use this key, you will find a blending of your inner and outer worlds. You'll find yourself filling with love. The teachings of ECK are all about God's love for you—and also how you can have true love for God.

People often feel that to truly love God means hating themselves. This isn't so. People cannot love God if they don't love themselves first.

It's almost a paradox: you can't love yourself until you love God, and you can't love God until you love yourself. You're like a hamster going around and around in a wheel. This wheel is called the wheel of reincarnation. Life after life you come back trying to solve the mystery, wondering how to love God, then how to love yourself.

The answer to that mystery is called spiritual freedom. And the way to spiritual freedom is simply to sing HU with love. That is where you begin.

That's the doorway to a new life, a life of love.

ECK European Seminar, Paris, France,
Saturday, July 25, 1992

Ready or not, the talk started coming through. She got a new title: "How to Get More Out of Your Daily Life: Learning to Recognize and Understand What Life Is Trying to Teach You."

14

Coming to ECK

A n ECKist has a cat named Humphrey. One evening the woman was lying on her bed reading *Child in the Wilderness,* a book I wrote about my experiences with the Light and Sound of God. As the woman got closer to the chapter on my experience with God-Realization on the bridge, Humphrey became very excited.

A Taste of ECK

He started running back and forth on the bed. Since it was a waterbed, this caused quite a commotion. Then Humphrey grew quiet and just sat on the bed looking up at the ceiling.

The ECKist looked up at the ceiling too, but she couldn't see anything. She wondered what had caused Humphrey's excitement. It was because the cat could feel what I was trying to put into the book. I wrote it as well as I could, thinking maybe someday somebody would understand. Maybe the cat did.

Cats have an ability to see into the other planes, into the Astral Plane. They can see the spiritual travelers who come and go from the Astral to the Causal, Mental, and higher. If they're friendly people, the cats are just interested; if they're frightening, the cats are frightened.

How do people come to ECK? In this case, the cat found out about ECK through his owner reading an ECK book.

Sharing Truth

A businesswoman in California got a call one day from a member of a Masonic group. He asked if she would give a talk; she had given talks before for the group, and they liked her. "I'm sorry it's only a week's notice," he apologized. The woman agreed anyway. After she hung up, she thought maybe this would be an opportunity to give a talk on the principles of ECK but not use ECKANKAR terms.

She knew that the Masonic group was interested in history, so she put together a talk on kingship beliefs, doing her research and taking notes. But the day before the talk was scheduled, the ECKist realized that it wasn't working. The material was good, but the talk wasn't working.

What bothered her most was that her communication with the Inner Master had stopped. She wasn't hearing the Sound of ECK anymore.

The woman decided to go to bed early that night and get up early in the morning to finalize her talk for the next day. She set her alarm for 4:00 a.m., a time she felt she was often at her creative best. Instead, she woke up at 2:00 a.m., very alert and wide awake.

Ready or not, the talk started coming through. She began to write down the points that came when suddenly she got a new title: "How to Get More Out of Your Daily Life: Learning to Recognize and Understand What Life Is Trying to Teach You."

This, she knew, would be her way of talking about ECK to these businessmen.

The points for her talk and the stories spilled out, one after another. She found stories from her personal life, waking dreams, things that had happened that were the Holy Spirit's way of telling her something significant for her spiritual unfoldment. Within an hour she had written a whole new talk.

But the woman was unsure. It was a big risk, giving a talk like this when the businesspeople were used to hearing her giving talks about university funds, about generating millions of dollars. So as she drove to the talk, she began chanting HU, this love song for God.

You Answered All My Questions

As she came in the door of the meeting hall, the person who had called her ran up to her. "We had you scheduled for thirty minutes," he said, "but can you do forty?" She said, "Yes, of course," even though this isn't something a speaker usually likes to hear. But as she sat in the business meeting that preceded her talk, she got two more examples of waking dreams. Each of these stories was worth five minutes, which covered her additional time.

As she gave the points in her talk, she noticed first one person then another nodding. When she finished, they gave her a standing ovation.

The most touching response came from a sixty-year-old gentleman. "I had so many questions," he said, "and you've answered many of them. Could you come back and speak to us again?"

This experience was an excellent example of how the woman could touch people who knew nothing about ECK but could feel the truth behind her words. She didn't have

179

to use ECK terms, like *SUGMAD,* yet they could tell she was speaking truth.

Long Road to Find ECK

Another person who came to ECK had a long road. When he was two or three, he used to lie in his crib looking out the window at the stars. One night he noticed that there was one star that began to move sideways, left to right, left to right. Suddenly the star came zooming toward earth and came right into his bedroom window.

The star became two stars, a blue one and a white one. An instant later, two spiritual travelers stood in his bedroom. One of them said, "Don't be afraid, we came to you because of your love."

The little boy climbed out of his crib to go wake his parents. As he walked over to his parents' bed, he heard one of the spiritual travelers say, "He's not ready yet." And they left.

The next time this person ran into a spiritual traveler was when he was out of high school, living in Indiana. He met a beggar, a tall man with clear, striking eyes, who said, "Could I borrow two dollars?"

The young man only had ten dollars on him but he said to the beggar, "Here, have three." "I only need two," said the man.

Then the man said, "In case you're interested, Paul Twitchell is giving a talk in town tonight." "What's he talking about?" asked the young man. When he found out it was about spiritual things, the young man decided the beggar was some kind of nut. "No thanks," he said.

But when the young man gave the beggar the money, the beggar said, "The blessings of God, the SUGMAD, are with you." The young man didn't realize this was a spiritual traveler in disguise. He had come to give the young man his second invitation to the teachings of ECK. But the young man had told him, "I'm not ready for this yet."

Accepting the Gift

The third time the young man came across the ECK teachings was as a soldier in Vietnam.

Gopal Das, an ECK Master who served as the Mahanta in Egypt many years ago, would take the soldier out of his body every night. They would go to a Golden Wisdom Temple in the higher planes of God where the young man attended classes.

But after a period of time, the young man got restless. He wanted to look around instead of just going to Satsang class.

Gopal Das said to him, "If you leave class, we won't meet again." And after that day he never met Gopal Das again. He feels he never will again in this lifetime, but he will when he's ready. He fell away from ECK for years, and recently he's come back again.

He realizes that he had the gift of traveling with this particular ECK Master but he hadn't recognized the gift, perhaps because he was too young. For whatever reason, he had turned his back on the teachings. But he's got them again now. And again the test will be Will he stay?

Right now he is in the middle of a test of faith, because people are coming up to him and trying to shake his faith in ECK.

We all face these challenges; I know I did. It's a spiritual shakeout, a consolidation time. Sometimes we grow very quickly and reach a new plateau, a new level of spiritual unfoldment. We reach that new level of the God Worlds we have visited in our dreams before. Now, in full awareness, we have to learn the rules of this particular plane of heaven. We have to learn the spiritual laws governing that plane.

Past Lives in Europe

Having the ECK European Seminar in a new city this year means that people will be working out their karma with this city.

We were in the Netherlands for ten years. As people work out their karma they go into past lives in the dream state. They find out what part they played in the history of northern Europe. Many of them helped build the country, sometimes fighting to defend their homeland.

You who are fortunate enough to come here may find images coming in your dreams about previous lives you spent here in France when it was called something else. You're going to see how you helped establish the foundations of history for this area. You helped build it, sometimes you even helped destroy it. These are the parts we play in history.

Sometimes we are more enamored by power than by love. During those lifetimes, we hurt many other people and the time comes to pay back our debt. Not to someone else but to ourselves. At other times we did great deeds of love instead of selfishness. We gained in our karmic balance sheet.

We bring these credits and debits into this lifetime.

The Best You Have Ever Been

You are now the most complete spiritual being you have ever been. Sometimes you may look at yourself and say, "I haven't come very far, have I?" But you are the best that you've ever been, and there's still a long way to go.

By the mere fact of being in ECK today you can break this cycle, the paradox or riddle of how do I love myself more to love God more? You can't do one without the other. Most people don't break through this riddle for lifetimes. It takes them in a circle, which becomes a wheel. We call it the wheel of reincarnation, the many lives we spend trying to get on top of things.

When the ECK Masters come to give us the invitation to break out of this prison we have created for ourselves, we may say, "No, thank you, I'm not ready yet."

No loss, because you just come when you're ready. You don't lose anything by coming to the path of ECK later. When you're tired of the experiences—of going through the emotional, mental, and physical pain—you've become a more refined spiritual being, more ready to serve God as a Co-worker. At this point, you'll say to the invitation, "Sure, I'd like to know more about ECK."

Then one of the ECK Masters or I will come to you.

An Inner Bond

Out here I give you the ECK writings, the teachings, the spiritual exercises. These are keys to unlocking your secret worlds. You've got to use them, and once you do you can have the help of the spiritual travelers.

The more enjoyable teachings come from the Inner Master. Once we establish an inner bond, which can only occur through agreement between you and me, we can work one-on-one. It requires your saying yes to the invitation. Then I can take you into past lives, and I can show you the future if needed.

But these things are not as important as showing you how to live in the present moment.

I Want Answers Now

A man joined the Pentecostal church in 1967 when he was living in Brooklyn, New York. He cared very much about God. But in his searchings and questionings, people would tell him, "You don't want to ask too many questions about God. You'll get answers when you die."

"But I want answers now," the man said.

"Have faith," they said.

About a year before he left the Pentecostal church, he began having experiences with the Light and Sound of God. He'd shut his eyes for ten minutes, and this beautiful light would come in different colors, mostly purple or gold. It looked like a whirlwind in the distance. He also began to hear an inner sound similar to crickets.

"What is this Light and Sound?" he asked the people in his church.

"Don't ask those things," they said. "Be filled with the Holy Ghost." The test for that church was to be able to speak in tongues, which is a lower form of experience with the Light and Sound of God. One Sunday when the minister asked those who could witness the Holy Ghost to come forward, the man stayed in his seat up in the balcony. He couldn't speak in tongues.

He shut his eyes, and the Blue Light came to him. Suddenly the purple light came into his vision, and he saw it falling like raindrops on the congregation. They were receiving the Light of God. The others felt It, but he actually saw It. Feeling is emotional, from the Astral Plane, which is where the people in the Pentecostal religion make their heaven.

Not long after, the man read the book *How to Find God*. It explained his experiences with the Light and Sound of God.

Soul's Many Experiences

When you come into ECK you realize that sometime in the past, you have had all these experiences in the different churches. Then you went on to another lifetime. Between lives, your spiritual guide is often the angel of karma who works with you until you're ready to enter the ECK teachings and work with one of the ECK Masters.

You realize when you come into ECK that there is no need to look down on any religious teaching. At one time, you were also a member of that sort of teaching, whether or not it has the same modern name today. This lifetime this particular man joined the Pentecostal church; two thousand years ago he may have joined the early Christian church.

Speaking in tongues was considered a high point in spiritual unfoldment for the people then. But today we recognize it as an elementary step. When you've gained all your experience at that level, you move on to something else. Maybe you'll even go through a period of being an atheist or agnostic.

Why? Because Soul wants those experiences. Otherwise, how can you serve people in this world?

Narrow-minded people of limited spiritual experience cannot serve God or others. They haven't learned to love themselves. When you realize you have had all these experiences, there's no reason to look down on other people because it would be looking down on yourself.

The Ocean of God

There are higher heavens. Christians make their heaven on the Mental Plane. In ECKANKAR, our heaven can be any one of the inner planes, because if you have finished experiences on the Astral Plane, you may go for a time to the Causal Plane or the Mental Plane. It doesn't make any difference. You are established on the Soul Plane, the true home of Soul. No forms exist there.

In Paul Twitchell's *The Tiger's Fang,* he speaks in terms of forms, people appearing at will. You can create a landscape at will. But the world itself exists as purely Light and Sound.

The Sound is actually a wave that goes out from the heart of God. It comes down through the heavens into the physical world, then It goes back to God. This is the wave Soul must catch at some time.

Like an ocean wave, It washes onto the shore, then the ripples go back out into the ocean and return to the heart of God. This is why we call God the Ocean of Love and Mercy. It's a metaphor, because you cannot explain God. This is the closest you can come.

"Amazing HU" Technique

I want to give you a spiritual exercise to help you reach greater spiritual freedom. It's tied to the song "Amazing HU," which we adapted from the public-domain song "Amazing Grace" by John Newton, the slave trader.

The words are as follows:

Amazing HU, how sweet the Sound,
That touched a Soul like me!
I once was lost, but now am found,
Was blind, but now I see.

'Twas HU that taught my heart to sing,
And HU my fears relieved;
How precious did HU then appear
The hour I first believed!

186

Through many dangers, toils, and snares,
        I have already come;
'Tis HU has brought me safe thus far,
        And HU will lead me home.

The HU has given life to me,
        Its Sound my hope secures;
My shield and portion HU will be
        As long as life endures.

The earth will someday pass away;
        The sun forbear to shine;
But God, who sent me here below,
        I'll be forever Thine.

A woman had a reaction to "Amazing HU" but instead of just hating it, she did something positive. She sat down and tried to memorize all the verses. Then a peculiar thing happened. The woman began having a past-life recall of when she was a black slave.

Not long after this, other people would mention to her how they had a problem with "Amazing HU." "You might try something: memorize the verses," she would tell them. She didn't say anything about her past-life recall, just told them to memorize the verses. One person came back to her and said, "I was having these memories of when I was an American Indian. I had all these past-life recalls of when I was a slave there."

Then another person came up to her. "I am now able to accept 'Amazing HU,' " he said, "but I had some interesting experiences."

"Did it have anything to do with a past life when you were a slave?" asked the woman.

"Yes, as a matter of fact, I had a past-life recall where I was an Egyptian slave," the other ECKist said. "How did you know?"

Letting Go of Victim Consciousness

There's a victim consciousness among some ECKists. If something doesn't go right, they want to blame someone else. It's easy to say, "Now I understand; it was because I was a slave. Somebody else took away my freedom."

But we forget that sometimes we were slaves because first we were the slave masters. It's that old circle again, the circle that holds us to the wheel. Slave master makes slaves, slave gets free, the slave becomes the slave master who makes slaves. Around and around we go. Where it stops, nobody knows.

Except you and I know. It can stop in this lifetime.

"Amazing HU" is a good technique for finding more spiritual freedom. Perhaps it will help you have past-life recalls where you were the slave or where you were the slave master. Where you took from life, and where you gave. Where you used power, and where you used love. The life you took, and the life you gave.

You'll find all this inside you.

ECK European Seminar, Paris, France,
Sunday, July 26, 1992

188

Glossary

Words set in SMALL CAPS are defined elsewhere in this glossary.

ARAHATA. An experienced and qualified teacher for ECKANKAR classes.

CHELA. A spiritual student.

ECK. The Life Force, the Holy Spirit, or Audible Life Current which sustains all life.

ECKANKAR. Religion of the Light and Sound of God. Also known as the Ancient Science of SOUL TRAVEL. A truly spiritual religion for the individual in modern times, known as the secret path to God via dreams and SOUL TRAVEL. The teachings provide a framework for anyone to explore their own spiritual experiences. Established by Paul Twitchell, the modern-day founder, in 1965.

ECK MASTERS. Spiritual Masters who can assist and protect people in their spiritual studies and travels. The ECK Masters are from a long line of God-Realized SOULS who know the responsibility that goes with spiritual freedom.

HU. The most ancient, secret name for God. The singing of the word HU, pronounced like the word *hue,* is considered a love song to God. It is sung in the ECK Worship Service.

INITIATION. Earned by the ECK member through spiritual unfoldment and service to God. The initiation is a private ceremony in which the individual is linked to the Sound and Light of God.

LIVING ECK MASTER. The title of the spiritual leader of ECKANKAR. His duty is to lead SOULS back to God. The Living ECK Master can assist spiritual students physically as the Outer Master, in the dream state as the Dream Master, and in the spiritual worlds as the

189

Inner Master. Sri Harold Klemp became the MAHANTA, the Living ECK Master in 1981.

MAHANTA. A title to describe the highest state of God Consciousness on earth, often embodied in the LIVING ECK MASTER. He is the Living Word.

PLANES. The levels of heaven, such as the Astral, Causal, Mental, Etheric, and Soul planes.

SATSANG. A class in which students of ECK study a monthly lesson from ECKANKAR.

THE SHARIYAT-KI-SUGMAD. The sacred scriptures of ECKANKAR. The scriptures are comprised of twelve volumes in the spiritual worlds. The first two were transcribed from the inner PLANES by Paul Twitchell, modern-day founder of ECKANKAR.

SOUL. The True Self. The inner, most sacred part of each person. Soul exists before birth and lives on after the death of the physical body. As a spark of God, Soul can see, know, and perceive all things. It is the creative center of Its own world.

SOUL TRAVEL. The expansion of consciousness. The ability of SOUL to transcend the physical body and travel into the spiritual worlds of God. Soul Travel is taught only by the LIVING ECK MASTER. It helps people unfold spiritually and can provide proof of the existence of God and life after death.

SOUND AND LIGHT OF ECK. The Holy Spirit. The two aspects through which God appears in the lower worlds. People can experience them by looking and listening within themselves and through SOUL TRAVEL.

SPIRITUAL EXERCISES OF ECK. The daily practice of certain techniques to get us in touch with the Light and Sound of God.

SUGMAD. A sacred name for God. SUGMAD is neither masculine nor feminine; IT is the source of all life.

WAH Z. The spiritual name of Sri Harold Klemp. It means the Secret Doctrine. It is his name in the spiritual worlds.

Index

Active, 54, 56
Activity. *See* Circles of activity
Africa, 13, 47, 102–4
Aging, 55–56
Agnostic(s), 80, 185
Airplane, 56–57
Alaska, 160–61
"Amazing HU," 186–87, 188
America, 7, 89, 170, 171
Angel(s), 47, 80, 107, 185
Anger, 119, 120, 155
Animals, 21, 85, 87. *See also*
    Apes; Birds; Blackbirds;
    Blue jays; Cardinal; Cat(s);
    Dog(s); Donald and Daisy;
    Dragonflies; Geese; Mosqui-
    toes; Mouse story; Peanut;
    Pets; Pheasant; Rabbit(s);
    Raccoons; Robin(s); Spar-
    rows; Spider; Squirrel(s);
    Sugarbear; Wolf
Animism, 92
Apes, 87, 102
Appreciation, 20, 164
Are You Being Served? 68, 70–80
Armageddon. *See* Judgment Day
Atheist(s), 80, 185
Attention, 55
Attitude, 54, 57
Authority, symbol of, 70, 71, 75
Awareness. *See also* Conscious-
    ness

gaining, 24
greater, 12
higher, 5, 30, 117
in the humble places, 26
through initiation, 134
of the inner worlds, 117, 131,
    182
of love, 35
of the presence of God, 161–62
of spiritual insight, 116
during waking life, 138, 162,
    167
of what you do, 6
of who you are, 8, 10, 12, 173

Beggar, 180
Being(s), spiritual, 5, 106, 153,
    156, 160, 182, 183. *See also*
    Human being(s)
Bells. *See* Sound: of bells
Bible, 49, 104, 106, 108, 133
Bicycle story, 138–41
Birds, 21, 85, 87
Blackbirds, 21
Blame (blaming), 8, 33, 45, 127,
    145, 156, 170, 188
Blessing(s)
    bringing, to us, 63, 101
    of God, 62, 180
    gratitude for, 11, 25
    pain as, 36
    recognizing, 25, 173

191

Blue jays, 21
Blue Star of ECK, 114. *See also*
    Light: Blue
Body, physical, 11, 111
Book of ECK Parables, The, 60
Books. *See* ECKANKAR: book
Buddhists, 92
Building blocks, 171. *See also*
    Stepping-stones

Cardinal, 1, 84
Cartoons, 68
Cat(s), 34–35, 88, 177–78
Catholic(s), 80, 111, 161
Cause and effect, 3–4, 57, 94
Challenge(s), 158, 181
Change, 36, 41, 57–58, 105, 134
Charity, 7
Cheesecake, 19
Child in the Wilderness, 177
Child of God, 12
Children (childhood), 5, 153,
    159–61
Choice(s), 90, 147
Christian(s) (Christianity), 132.
    See also Bible; Catholic(s);
    Jesus Christ; Lutherans;
    Pentecostal church; Saint
    Paul
  early, 22, 104, 185
  ECKANKAR and. *See*
  ECKANKAR: and Chris-
    tianity
  heaven of, 185
  and the Holy Spirit, 46, 94
  past lives as, 92
  and spiritual community, 67
Circles of activity, 128–29
Clock, 46
Communication, 95. *See also*
    Miscommunication; Speak-
    ers (speaking); Talk(s);
    Write (writers)
Community, 67–80, 114
Compassion, 31, 80
Complaining, 124–25, 127, 171

Complication, 71
Computers, 99–100, 129
Conclusions, wrong, 158
Confidence, 24, 61, 106, 151
Consciousness, 22, 23, 117, 126,
    147, 173. *See also* Uncon-
    sciousness
Contemplation, 24, 46, 90, 94.
    See also Spiritual Exercises
    of ECK
Conveniences, modern, 13, 48
Courage, 24, 58, 89, 150
Co-worker with God, 58, 72, 80,
    171, 183
Creation, 94
Creativity, 143, 156, 171

Dark Night of Soul, 128
Day, ordinary, story 31–33
Death, 111, 132–33
Debt, 13, 153, 182. *See also*
    Karma
Decisions, 162
Deeds, 54
Dentist, 31–32, 153
Depression, 107, 152
Despair, 48
Destiny, 23, 58
Diet, 31, 170
Dignity, 77–78, 79
Direction, 117–18
Disneyland, 102
Divine (divinity), 12. *See also*
    Spirit, Divine
  influence, 101
  power, 71
Doctor, 41, 153. *See also* Dentist
Dog(s), 88, 119–20, 162–63
Dogma, 105, 106
Doing something well, 44, 142–44
Donald and Daisy, 98–99
Donations, 62–63
Doorway, 165, 174
Dragonflies, 17–18
Dream(s)
  building your, 48, 101

192

journal, 116
learning through, 4, 24, 31, 36, 115, 135
Master works through, 8, 47, 58, 104
past life experience in, 182
reality of, worlds, 117, 137–38
remembering, 13, 23–24, 30, 61, 131
symbolism, 23, 116–17
testing your, 106, 118
visiting inner worlds through, 30, 89, 181
Dream Master, 23–24, 31
Dress story, 36–39
Drum. *See* Sound: of a drum
Ducks. *See* Donald and Daisy

Ear, 172–73
Earth, 22, 48, 134, 144, 155
ECK. *See also* ECKANKAR: teachings
coming to, 180–81, 183, 185
faith in, 181
help of, 49, 59, 155–56
as inner teaching, 58, 183
life in, 12–13, 23, 35, 55, 101
nature of, 29, 94, 107, 143
principles of, 76, 100
riches of, 113, 115, 116–17, 120
talking about, 99, 100, 178–80
will of, 101
ECKANKAR
aspects of, 4
book, 4, 178. *See also Book of ECK Parables, The; Child in the Wilderness; How to Find God,* Mahanta Transcripts, Book 2; *Tiger's Fang, The*
and Christianity, 1
coming to, 60, 130–31, 146, 150
discourses, 24
heaven for, 185–86

and the individual, 78, 156
life in, 147
members of, 130, 131, 134, 172. *See also* ECKist(s)
and realizing God's gifts, 128
and responsibility, 6, 36
seminars. *See* Seminar(s), ECK
and Soul, 111
teachings, 11–12, 13, 54, 61, 102, 112–13, 126, 129, 131, 134, 173, 181, 185
terms, 129, 178
ECKANKAR Journal, The, 31
ECKist(s), 80, 107, 124, 130, 177, 188
ECK Master(s), 61, 104, 131, 183, 185. *See also* Dream Master; Fubbi Quantz; Gopal Das; Inner Master; Living ECK Master; Mahanta; Master(s)(ship); Outer Master; Rebazar Tarzs; Twitchell, Paul
ECK Stream, 120. *See also* Light and Sound (of God)
ECK-Vidya, 42. *See also* Prophecy
Effort, 23, 101, 169
Emotions, 12, 184
Entitlements, 169–70
Expectations, 44, 48–49, 69
Experience(s)
benefiting from others', 120
in different churches, 185
inner, 30, 47, 57, 61
learning from, 35–36, 138, 160, 162
life, 164
mystical, 29
spiritual, 124, 131, 164
tired of, 183
Experiment, 100–101
Expert, 4, 142, 144, 146
Explorers, 89
Eyes, 25, 92

193

will of, 11
will show you love, 39
God Consciousness, 85
God-Realization, 177
Golden heart, 156, 162
Golden Wisdom Temple, 181
Gopal Das, 181
Government, 143, 169–70
Graduation, 5
Gratitude, 11, 33. *See also*
 Blessing(s): gratitude for
Growth, spiritual, 61, 63
 through attention on God, 33
 through inner experience, 138
 others interfering with, 145–
 46
 as our purpose here, 59
 pace of, 181
 through serving God, 144
 and spiritual community, 68,
 137

Handouts, 143
Happy (happiness), 18, 33, 48,
 54, 63, 127, 160
Hardship(s), 33, 83, 124, 171.
 See also Problem(s)
Hawaii, 91
Hay fever, 8–9
Healing(s), 11, 153, 173
Health, 31, 44, 48
Heart, 22, 101, 134, 164
Heaven(s), 58, 111
 creating, 57
 levels of, 117, 185–86
 nature of, 30, 182
 as other worlds, 151
 of Pentecostal church. *See*
 Pentecostal church
 reach, 104–5, 156
Help, 97, 104, 114, 156, 170. *See
 also* ECK: help of; God: help
 from; HU: help through
Hierarchy, 68, 70–71
Higher Initiate(s), 90, 100, 131

Hindu(s), 67, 161
History, 182
Holidays, 170
Holy Spirit. *See also* ECK
 creative power of, 171
 definition of, 46, 94, 167
 how the, works, 100–101
 as Light and Sound, 133, 168
 and love, 57, 61, 91
 richness of, 63
 teaches us, 60, 105, 179
Hope(s), 44, 95
How to Find God, Mahanta
 Transcripts, Book 2, 184
HU
 awareness through, 173
 brings Light and Sound, 168
 chanting, 179
 help through, 60, 63, 107, 171
 as name for God, 95, 105, 168
 power and love in, 51, 108
 purpose of, 11, 55, 100, 126
 singing, 63
 as spiritual exercise, 90, 94,
 105, 107–8, 133
 and spiritual freedom, 135,
 174
 telling others about, 100
 understanding through, 95,
 106
 uplifts, 14
 when in trouble, 13, 51, 95,
 102–3, 105
Human
 consciousness, 22
 nature, 7, 8
 race, 6–7
 self, 24
Human being(s), 153
 behavior of, 21–22, 87
 each, is special, 12
 and family, 159–60
 limitations of, 60
 origins of, 102
 and survival, 94
Humility, 26, 116

Ice cream, 168
Illness, 8, 11, 44–45, 104
Illusion, 44, 45, 48, 158
Independence, 113, 160
Individual(s), 11, 77–78, 79
Initiate report, 151–52, 153
Initiates, ECK, 116, 137. *See also* ECKist(s)
Initiation
  Eighth, 18–19
  First, 134
  Second, 134
Initiative, 57
Initiator, ECK, 134
Inner Master. *See also* Mahanta
  asking the, 114
  communication with, 90, 178
  instruction from, 115–16, 183
  learning from, 89
  message from, 164–65
Insight, 51, 95, 116, 131, 171
Intuition, 36, 104
Investments, 118

Jacket, 18
Jains, 92
Japan, 169
Jesus Christ, 6, 46, 47, 132. *See also* Christian(s) (Christianity)
Jews, 67
Job, 8, 114–15
Journal, 116
Joy, 25, 163, 164
Judgment Day, 5–7, 21–22
Justice, 78–79

Karma, 17
  angel of, 185
  nature of, 1, 7, 22–23, 76, 80
  unwinding, 10, 153
  working out, 13, 182
Knowledge (knowing), 29, 117, 131

Laughter, 163–64
Law(s)
  of Karma, 22–23, 80
  of Plenty, 63–64
  of prosperity, 62
  spiritual, 23, 170, 182
Leader(ship), 22, 73, 78, 115
Learn(ing), 4, 58–59, 88, 89, 160, 167. *See also* Lesson(s)
Legacy, spiritual, 117
Lesson(s)
  of freedom, 141, 144, 146
  from nature, 87
  in other worlds, 138
  about power, 91
  of this life, 158, 162, 171
Levitation, 104
Life (lives) (living). *See also* ECK: life in
  accept, 33
  building your, 49, 63
  changing, 134, 143
  close to, 13
  continuity of, 30
  create a better, 11, 24, 31, 39, 147
  cutting edge of, 100
  daily, 8, 29, 34–35, 115
  dealing with, 147, 151
  divine influence in your, 101
  easy, 158
  enjoying, 10, 58
  fully, 101
  getting along in, 87
  getting rid of unnecessary things in, 83
  hard, 23, 55
  help in daily, 97, 107
  holistic, 135
  in the Holy Spirit, 57
  is worth living, 97
  learning from, 60, 138, 178–79
  and Light and Sound, 94, 164
  living, fully, 57, 172
  of love, 22, 63, 165, 174
  nature of, 90, 94, 128

on other planets, 128
past. *See* Past: life
 as a projection screen, 171–72
 purpose in, 35, 59, 171
 richer, 23, 35
 seeing, 42, 48
 taking charge of your, 23, 51,
  57–58, 61
 truly, 12
 we create our, 33, 54
 what, has to offer, 53, 169
 what, requires of us, 160
Light
 Blue, 184
 experience with, 132–33
 look for, 95
 nature of, 94, 133–34
 people need, 107
Light and Sound (of God). *See*
  also ECK; Holy Spirit;
  Light; Sound; Spirit, Divine
 as aspects of God, 46
 experience with, 31, 92–94,
  131, 172–73, 177, 184
 God speaks through, 29,
  106–7, 167
 life could not exist without, 94,
  164
 nature of, 94, 164–65
 and other teachers, 106, 133
 and shutters around Soul, 168
 telling people about, 100
Limitations, 60
Listening, 68
Living ECK Master, 41, 89, 134.
  See also Mahanta
Loneliness, 35, 38, 39
Love (divine), 56, 115
 accepting, 146–48
 as attribute of God, 7
 deeds of, 182
 desire for, 147
 doing something for, 18, 114,
  142–44
 expression of, 107, 165
 filling with, 31, 173

freedom brings, 155
giving, 35, 63, 114, 117, 120
of God, 19, 20, 22, 24–26, 31,
 33, 35, 51, 57, 147–48, 165,
 173–74, 183
greater, 132, 146
learning, 39, 80
life, 57
looking for, 25–26, 33, 61
nature of, 39, 88, 107, 164–65
and pain, 35
and power, 91, 188
receiving God's, 134–35, 151
in the small things, 25–26, 33
spirit of, 156
true, 12, 19
wave of, 24
wrong kind of, 91
yourself, 173–74, 183, 185
Lutherans, 80, 161

Machines, 112–13
Mahanta. *See also* Dream
  Master; Inner Master;
  Living ECK Master
 guidance of, 24, 114–15
 presence of, 104
 reality of, 133
 works with us, 47, 150–53
Marriage, 44–45
Martyrs, 22
Master(s)(ship), 47, 130, 133,
  134, 151. *See also* ECK
  Master(s); Self-: mastery
Materialism (material things),
  49, 56, 141
Men, 112–13
Message, 22
Messenger, 47
Mexico, 169
Mind, 12, 13–14, 86
Miracles, 104, 173
Miscommunication, 69, 72, 74
Missionaries, 91–92
Momentum, 60–61
Money, 49, 117

200

201

How to Take the Next Step on Your Spiritual Journey

Find your own answers to questions about your past, present, and future through the ancient wisdom of ECKANKAR. Take the next bold step on your spiritual journey.

ECKANKAR can show you why special attention from God is neither random nor only for a few saints. It is for anyone who opens his heart to Divine Spirit, the Light and Sound of God.

Are you looking for the secrets of life and the afterlife? Sri Harold Klemp, today's spiritual leader of ECKANKAR, and Paul Twitchell, its modern-day founder, have written a series of monthly discourses that give unique Spiritual Exercises of ECK. They can lead you in a direct way to God. Those who join ECKANKAR, Religion of the Light and Sound of God, can receive these monthly discourses.

As a Member of ECKANKAR You'll Discover

1. The most direct route home to God through the ECK teachings of the Light and Sound. Plus the opportunity to gain wisdom, charity, and spiritual freedom in this lifetime through the ECK initiations.

2. The spiritual meaning of dreams, Soul Travel techniques, and ways to establish a personal relationship with Divine Spirit through study of monthly discourses. These discourses are for the entire family. You may study them alone at home or in a class with others.

3. Secrets of self-mastery in a Wisdom Note and articles by the Living ECK Master in the *Mystic World,* a quarterly newsletter. In it are also letters and articles from ECK members around the world.

4. Upcoming ECK seminars and other activities worldwide, new study materials from ECKANKAR, and more, in special mailings. Join the excitement. Have the fulfilling experience of attending major ECK seminars!

5. The joy of the ECK Satsang (discourse study) experience in classes and book discussions. Share spiritual experiences and find answers to your questions about the ECK teachings.

How to Find Out More

To request membership in ECKANKAR using your credit card (or for a free booklet on membership) call (612) 544-0066, weekdays, between 8:00 a.m. and 5:00 p.m., central time. Or write to: ECKANKAR, Att: Information, P.O. Box 27300, Minneapolis, MN 55427 U.S.A.

Introductory Books on ECKANKAR

The Drumbeat of Time
Mahanta Transcripts, Book 10
Harold Klemp

> You march through life to the drumbeat of time. Each drumbeat, each moment, each challenge you face is a chance to grow stronger in spirit.

This highly readable, sensible guide to living each moment fully is packed with Harold Klemp's stories, insights, and spiritual exercises.

ECKANKAR—Ancient Wisdom for Today

> Are you one of the millions who have heard God speak to you through a profound spiritual experience? This introductory book will show you how dreams, Soul Travel, and experiences with past lives are ways God speaks to you. An entertaining, easy-to-read approach

to ECKANKAR. Reading this little book can give you new perspectives on your spiritual life.

Stories to Help You See God in Your Life
The Book of ECK Parables, Volume 4
Harold Klemp

> Harold Klemp masterfully weaves parable after parable out of the most humble of circumstances. He shows us how to look for God in the little things. In this

book you'll discover how to listen to God, better understand your dreams and your relationships with others, and recognize the miracles in your life.

HU: A Love Song to God
(Audiocassette)

> Learn how to sing an ancient name for God, HU (pronounced like the word *hue*). A wonderful introduction to ECKANKAR, this two-tape set is designed to help listeners of any religious or philosophical back-

ground benefit from the gifts of the Holy Spirit. It includes an explanation of the HU, stories about how Divine Spirit works in daily life, and exercises to uplift you spiritually.

For fastest service, phone (612) 544-0066 weekdays between 8 a.m. and 5 p.m., central time, to request books using your credit card, or look under **ECKANKAR** in your phone book for an ECKANKAR Center near you. Or write: **ECKANKAR, Att: Information, P.O. Box 27300, Minneapolis, MN 55427 U.S.A.**

There May Be an
ECKANKAR Study Group near You

ECKANKAR offers a variety of local and international activities for the spiritual seeker. With hundreds of study groups worldwide, ECKANKAR is near you! Many areas have ECKANKAR Centers where you can browse through the books in a quiet, unpressured environment, talk with others who share an interest in this ancient teaching, and attend beginning discussion classes on how to gain the attributes of Soul: wisdom, power, love, and freedom.

Around the world, ECKANKAR study groups offer special one-day or weekend seminars on the basic teachings of ECKANKAR. Check your phone book under **ECKANKAR**, or call **(612) 544-0066** for membership information and the location of the ECKANKAR Center or study group nearest you. Or write **ECKANKAR, Att: Information, P.O. Box 27300, Minneapolis, MN 55427 U.S.A.**

☐ Please send me information on the nearest ECKANKAR Center or study group in my area.

☐ Please send me more information about membership in ECKANKAR, which includes a twelve-month spiritual study.

Please type or print clearly   814

Name _____

Street_____ Apt. # _____

City _____ State/Prov. _____

ZIP/Postal Code _____ Country _____